Social Service
Resource Guide
Oklahoma

Williams Commercial Group, LLC
PO Box 2075
Broken Arrow, OK 74013

Ordering Information:

Quantity sales. Special discounts are available on quantity purchases by corporations, associations, and others.
For details, contact the publisher at the address above.
Orders by U.S. trade bookstores and wholesalers.
Call:
(888)654-3129

Printed in the United States of America

Oklahoma's Cost of Living:

- The median sales price of a home in Oklahoma is $137,000 – among the lowest in the country. In Oklahoma, you can have your dream home for half of what it would cost in a coastal market.

- Basic utility costs are below the national average in Oklahoma. For example, Oklahoma City utility costs are 20 percent less than Dallas'. That means Oklahomans have more money for retirement nest eggs, paying off mortgages or taking vacations.

- In Oklahoma, gasoline costs 7 percent less than the national average.

- Rent in Oklahoma is about 25 percent cheaper than the national average.

Oklahoma's Quality of Life:

We offer a wide variety of outdoor recreation – according to the Environmental Protection Agency, Oklahoma is one of only four states to have ten or more "eco-regions," or areas that have a distinct terrain.

- Oklahoma has more than 300 museums covering a wide variety of subjects, from the Philbrook Museum of Art in Tulsa to Oklahoma City's National Cowboy and Western Heritage Museum.

- Oklahoma is home to one of the nation's best professional sports franchises – the Oklahoma City Thunder – according to ESPN The Magazine's 2013 "Ultimate Standings" article.

- Oklahoma boasts more than 11,600 miles of shoreline and more than 78,500 miles of rivers and streams.

- Our major metropolitan areas – Oklahoma City, Tulsa and Lawton – are growing and improving their quality of life each year.

Contents

SOCIAL SERVICE RESOURCE GUIDE *OKLAHOMA* 1

ABOUT US 10

AFFORDABLE CARE.. 11

MARKETPLACE 101 12

UNDERSTAND THE HEALTH INSURANCE MARKETPLACE................... 12

DATES & DEADLINES FOR 2016 HEALTH INSURANCE...................... 37

HEALTH INSURANCE MARKETPLACETIPS 37

DENTAL COVERAGE IN THE MARKETPLACE 41

Adult and Child Dental Insurance in the Marketplace 42

HOW TO ENROLL IN THE S.H.O.P. MARKETPLACE.......................... 42

PATIENT PROTECTION AND AFFORDABLE CARE ACT: 47

Option 1: Your Employer Plan 48

Option 2 – The Health Insurance Marketplace............................ 49

OKLAHOMA HEALTH CARE 50

MEDICAL PROGRAMS CONTACT: 50

SOONER CARE (OKLAHOMA MEDICAID) 50

SOONER CARE PROGRAMS.. 51

InSure Oklahoma 51

Oklahoma Cares 52

SoonerCare Health Management Program-chronic Disease 52

SoonerCare Supplemental –Co-Insurance 52

SoonerCare Traditional - Institutionalized...*53*

SoonerPlan –Family Plaming..*53*

SoonerRide *53*

SoonerCare Choice-Medical Home Provider.......................*53*

TEFRA (TAX EQUITY AND FISCAL RESPONSIBILITY ACT OF 1982), ...53

CHILDREN'S HEALTH COVERAGE PROGRAMS IN OKLAHOMA..........................53

Medicaid and CHIP *53*

Dental Care...*54*

DOMESTIC VIOLENCE SURVIVOR 55

SURVIVOR WITNESS COORDINATOR 55

EMPLOYMENT RIGHTS TO SURVIVOR OF VIOLENT CRIME, ...59

KNOW YOUR RIGHTS AS A SURVIVOR OF A VIOLENT CRIME:.........................60

WHAT TYPE OF FINANCIAL ASSISTANCE MAY BE AVAILABLE FOR SURVIVORS OF VIOLENT CRIME? 63

EDUCATION OUTREACH 64

OUTREACH CENTER 64

TCC's Education Outreach Center....................................*64*

Union Public Schools:...*65*

EMPLOYMENT WORKFORCE DEVELOPMENT 67

YOUTH WORKFORCE DEVELOPMENT 67

WIA Youth Service Providers *68*

INCENTIVES FOR EMPLOYERS 71

Work Opportunity Tax Credit 71

Special Excepted Appointment (SEA) Project-Hire People with
Disabilities 73

Federal Bonding- "At-risk", Hard-to-place Job Seekers 74

Adult and Dislocated Worker 75

Work-Based Training, Age 55 and Older.................................. 76

EMPLOYMENT AND CAREER WEBSITE: 77

ONLINE CAREER ASSESSMENTS: 77

REGISTERED APPRENTISHIP PROGRAMS:....................................... 77

Locate Apprentiship Programs in Your State: 78

Veterans in Apprenticeship 79

FARMWORKER'S EMPLOYMENT RIGHTS... 79

National Monitor Advocate.. 80

Housing Opportunities for Farmworkers 80

FAIR HOUSING 83

WHAT PROFESSIONALS NEED TO KNOW ABOUT FAIR HOUSING...................... 83

Fair Housing Compliance Checklist....................................... 85

Create a Fair Housing Policy Statement 85

WHAT CONSUMERS NEED TO KNOW ABOUT THE FAIR HOUSING ACT 86

Where Your Rights Violated? 86

Additional Protection if You Have a Disability........................... 87

IN THE SALE AND RENTAL OF HOUSING: 88

Refuse to Make a Mortgage Loan.. 89

In Buildings That are Ready for First Occupancy After March 13, 1991, and Have an Elevator and Four or More Units:..................... 89

Housing Opportunities for Families... 90

IF YOU THINK YOUR RIGHTS HAVE BEEN VIOLATED 91

If You're Disabled: 91

Complaint Referrals.. 92

Contact Information 95

ONLINE CIVIL RIGHTS COMPLAINT FORM: 96

ONLINE FAIR HOUSING COMPLAINT FORM: 96

MENTAL HEALTH AND SUBSTANCE ABUSE SERVICES 99

VETERANS 136

HEALTH COVERAGE FOR MILITARY VETERANS 136

If You're A Veteran Without VA Health Care,............................... 141

If Your Dependents Are not Covered 141

HOMELESS VETS HEALTHCARE.. 142

VETERANS HOUSING FORECLOSURE PREVENTION 142

VETERANS EMPLOYMENT SERVICE REPRESENTATIVES (LVER) 143

Disabled Veterans Outreach Program Specialists (DVOP) 143

GENERAL RESOURCE DIRECTORY... 148

RESOURCE REFERRAL 148

CLOTHING 148

DIAPERS.. 153

CRISIS LINES AND HOTLINES AIDS/HIV 154

EMERGENCY SHELTER.. 156

HOUSING 158

HOMELESS DROP IN CENTERS.. 160

HOME IMPROVEMENT/ACCESSIBILITY 161

HOME PURCHASE/HOUSING COUNSELING/FORECLOSURE ASSISTANCE 162

LANDLORD/TENANT ASSISTANCE 164

LEGAL AID SERVICES OF OKLAHOMA - TULSA 164

SUPPORTIVE SERVICES FOR VETERAN FAMILIES 164

HOUSING SEARCH AND INFORMATION 165

LOW-INCOME/SUBSIDIZED RENTAL HOUSING 165

RENT PAYMENT ASSISTANCE 166

UTILITY ASSISTANCE.. 167

SPOTLIGHT DENTAL & HEALTHCARE 171

DISCOUNT DENTAL & HEALTH PLANS 171

GRASSROOTS HEALTHCARE 171

UNITED WAY PARTNER AGENCIES 173

SCHOOL DISTRICTS & PHONE 182

STATE AGENCIES 197

THE AUTHOR... 198

PRAYER OF SALVATION: 199

YOUR NEW LIFE: 200

MY PRAYER FOR YOU: 201

GUARANTEE 202

ADDICTIONS 202

DELIVERANCE FROM HARASSMENT 203

DEPRESSION 204

FAMILY 205

FEAR 206

FILLING OF HOLY SPIRIT 207

FINANCES / JOBS 209

FORGIVENESS.. 209

GUIDANCE... 210

HEALTH 211

MARRIAGE / COMPANIONSHIP 212

SALVATION / GOD'S LOVE....................................... 213

STRENGTH TO DO GOD'S WILL 214

About Us

Make A' Move Housing Association

Make A' Move Housing Association is a leading advocate for uncompensatable social support. The company helps patients in need find solutions for their care. Make A' Move Housing Association has served as an advocate for individuals, working in concert with social services agencies in securing adequate support, which supports the overall goal of reform: to ensure access to affordable solutions. Make A' Move Housing Association's mission with this program is to help hospitals and treat patients with compassion, dignity and respect.

After a comprehensive review process, Make A Move Housing Association, has been approved by the Centers for Medicare and Medicaid Services (CMS) to be a Certified Application Counselor Designated Organization (CDO). This designation expands our company's service offering to educate and certify consumers about healthcare options available through the Marketplaces.

This designation by CMS recognizes our unwavering commitment to ensure the successful implementation of the Affordable Care Act (ACA) through the positive engagement of patients who are eligible for new forms of coverage. On behalf of hospital clients and in support of their patients, Make A' Move Housing Association will provide services that help individual patients understand, apply and enroll for health coverage through all of the newly-established ACA Marketplaces, including federally facilitated, State partnership and state-based Marketplaces.

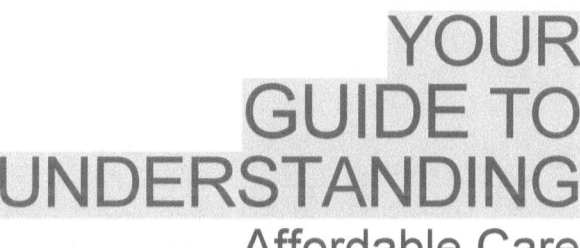

YOUR GUIDE TO UNDERSTANDING
Affordable Care

Logon to <u>www.makeamovehousing.org</u> to view:

- Publications:
    - <u>Your Health Plan and You - Know Your Health Coverage Protections</u>
- Webcasts
    - <u>Mujeres: aprovechen al máximo su cobertura médica archivo</u>
    - <u>The Affordable Care Act: How Will It Affect You?</u>
- Videos
    - <u>Health Care Coverage - Pay a Little to Save a Lot</u>
    - <u>Know Your Health Benefit Rights</u>
    - <u>Conozca Sus Derechos de Beneficios de Salud</u>

National Help and Medical Coverages:

If you are not a resident of Oklahoma go to the link below to find coverage and help in your State. http://insurekidsnow.gov/state/index.html

Marketplace 101

Marketplace 101

Find health care options that meet your needs and fit your budget

March 2016

Understand The Health Insurance Marketplace

- Understand and Explain the Health Insurance Marketplace

- Define who might be eligible

- Define options for those with limited income

- Explain the enrollment process

- Explain available options for people with Medicare

- Locate resources

What are Health Insurance Marketplaces?

- Created by the Affordable Care Act
- Where qualified individuals and families can directly compare private health insurance options
  - Known as qualified health plans (QHPs)
  - Can directly compare on the basis of price, benefits, quality, and other factors
- Also known as Exchanges
- Small Business Health Options Program (SHOP)
  - Marketplace for small employers
  - Provides coverage for their employees

How Health Insurance Marketplaces Work

- It uses one process to determine eligibility for
  - Qualified health plans through the Marketplaces
    - Premium tax credits to lower monthly premiums
    - Reduced cost sharing
  - Medicaid
  - Children's Health Insurance Program (CHIP)
- It offers choice of plans and levels of coverage
- Insurance companies compete for business

Marketplace Establishment

- Each state can decide to
  - Create and run a State-based Marketplace
  - Have a Marketplace operated by the federal government (Federally-Facilitated Marketplace)
  - Engage actively with the federal government in operating certain Marketplace functions (State-Partnership Marketplace)

Qualified Health Plans (QHPs)

- A QHP
  - Is offered through the Marketplace by an issuer that is licensed by the state and in good standing
  - Covers essential health benefits
  - Is offered by an issuer that offers at least one plan at the "Silver" and one at the "Gold" plan category of actuarial value
  - Charges same premium whether offered through a Marketplace or outside a Marketplace

Qualified Health Plans Cover
Essential Health Benefits

- Essential health benefits include at least these 10 categories
  - Ambulatory patient services
  - Emergency services
  - Hospitalization
  - Maternity and newborn care
  - Mental health and substance use disorder services, including behavioral health treatment
  - Prescription drugs
  - Rehabilitative and habilitative services and devices
  - Laboratory services
  - Preventive and wellness services and chronic disease management
  - Pediatric services, including oral and vision care (pediatric oral services may be provided by stand-alone plan)

Health Plan Categories

Lowest Premiums   **Highest Premiums**
Highest Out-of-Pocket Costs   **Lowest Out-of-Pocket Costs**

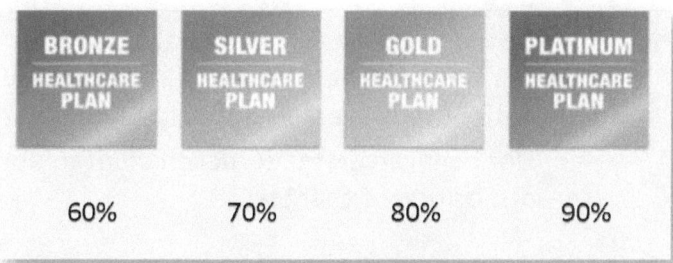

BRONZE	SILVER	GOLD	PLATINUM
HEALTHCARE PLAN	HEALTHCARE PLAN	HEALTHCARE PLAN	HEALTHCARE PLAN
60%	70%	80%	90%

Average Percentage of Covered Care Paid By the Plan

Catastrophic Health Plans

- What is catastrophic coverage?
  - Plans with high deductibles and lower premiums
  - You pay all medical costs for covered care up to the annual limit or cost sharing for the plan year
  - Includes 3 primary care visits per year and certain recommended preventive services with no out-of-pocket costs
  - Protects you from high out-of-pocket costs
- Who is eligible?
  - Young adults under 30 at the time they enroll or those who qualify for a hardship exemption

Eligibility and Enrollment in the Individual Market

- To be eligible for Marketplace coverage, you must
  - Be a resident of a state served by the Marketplace, and
  - Be a U.S. citizen, U.S. national, or a non-citizen who's lawfully present in the U.S. (and expected to be for the entire time coverage is sought), and
  - Not be incarcerated (other than incarceration pending disposition of charges)

Lower Premium Costs

- The premium tax credit may be taken as advance payments (APTC) paid directly to issuers to lower monthly premium costs, or as a refundable credit on the tax return you file
- Eligibility for APTC is based on
  - Household income and family size
    - Household income between 100% to 400% FPL
      - $24,250 – $97,00 for a family of 4 in 2016 (higher in Alaska and Hawaii)
  - Not being eligible for other minimum essential coverage, and including most government-sponsored coverage, affordable employer-sponsored insurance that meets certain minimum standards, or certain other minimum essential coverage

Ways to Use a Premium Tax Credit

Choose to Get It Now:
Advance Payments of the Premium Tax Credit (APTC)

- All or some of the APTC is paid directly to your plan on a monthly basis
- You pay the difference between the monthly premium and APTC
- You reconcile the APTC when you file a tax return for the coverage year*

Choose to Get It Later

- Don't request any advance payments
- You pay the entire monthly plan premium
- Claim the full amount on the tax return filed for the coverage year

You should report all changes in the information you provided on your application to avoid owing money, if you got more PTC then you were eligible for, after reconciliation on your tax return. Or, you could get money back or credited against any tax you may owe if you didn't get all the PTC for which you were eligible.

Who's Eligible for Cost-Sharing Reductions?

- Lower out-of-pocket costs on deductibles, copayments, and coinsurance
- To be eligible, you must
  - Have income at or below 250% FPL
    - $60,625 annually for a family of 4 in 2016 (higher in Alaska and Hawaii)
  - Be eligible for advance payments of the premium tax credit
  - **Enroll in a Marketplace Silver-level plan, unless they're members of a Federally-recognized tribe**
- Members of federally recognized Indian tribes
  - Don't have to pay cost-sharing if household income is at or below 300% of the federal poverty level (FPL), and they're eligible for advance payment of the premium tax credit
    - Up to around $72,750 for a family of 4 ($90,960 in Alaska) in 2016
    - Don't have to enroll in a Silver-level plan

Medicaid Eligibility

- Eligibility tied to groups specified under the federal Medicaid law
  - Pregnant women
  - Children
  - People with disabilities
  - Seniors
  - Parents and caretaker relatives
- States must cover certain groups, such as children and pregnant women, and have the option to cover other groups, such as childless adults
- Financial and non-financial requirements

Eligibility—Medicaid Expansion

- Affordable Care Act's Eligibility Groups
  1. Adult group
     - 19-64 with income below 133% of FPL
  2. Former foster care group
     - Under 26 and enrolled in Medicaid while in foster care at 18 or "aged out" of foster care (no income test)
  3. Optional eligibility group for individuals with income above 133% of FPL
     - Under 65 with income above 133% of FPL
- 12-month eligibility period for most adults, parents, and children

Application and Eligibility

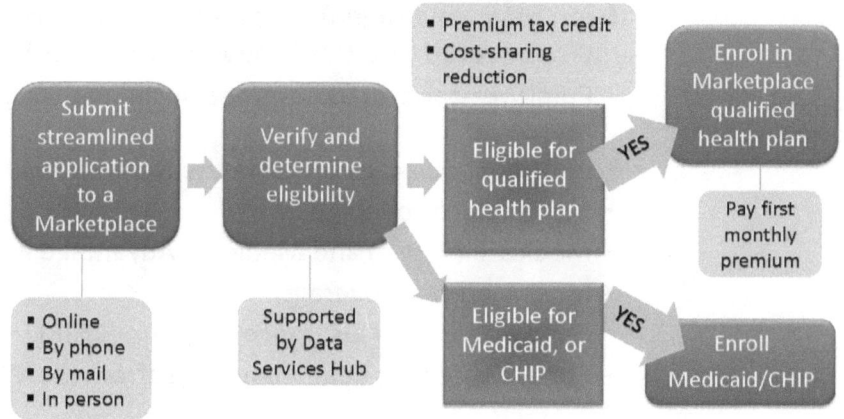

Everyone Must:

1. Have minimum essential coverage **OR**	2. Have an exemption from the shared responsibility payment (fee) **OR**	3. Pay a fee (shared responsibility payment)
	EXEMPT	
They're already covered and don't need to do anything.	They don't have to get coverage and won't have to pay a fee for not having coverage.	They should consider getting coverage. If they don't, they'll pay a fee.

1. What is Minimum Essential Coverage?

- If you have coverage from any of the following, you're covered and **don't have to do anything**
  - Employer-sponsored coverage, including COBRA and retiree
  - Individual coverage (outside the Marketplace)
  - Marketplace coverage
  - Medicare (Part A) and Medicare Advantage Plans
  - Most Medicaid coverage
  - Children's Health Insurance Program (CHIP)
  - Certain veteran's health coverage (from the VA)

What is Minimum Essential Coverage? Continued

- If you have coverage from any of the following, you have minimum essential coverage
  - Most types of TRICARE coverage
  - Coverage provided to Peace Corp volunteers
  - Coverage under the Nonappropriated Fund Health Benefit Program
  - Refugee Medical Assistance (ACF)
  - Self-funded health coverage offered to students by universities
  - State high risk pools
  - Other coverage recognized by the Secretary of HHS

2. Who is Eligible for an Exemption?

- You are eligible to receive an exemption if you [EXEMPT]
  - Are a member of a recognized religious sect with religious objections to insurance
  - Are a member of a recognized health care sharing ministry
  - Are a member of a federally recognized tribe or eligible for services through an Indian Health Services provider
  - Don't make the minimum income required to file taxes

Who is Eligible for an Exemption? Continued

- You may be eligible for an exemption if you   EXEMPT
    - Had a short coverage gap (less than 3 consecutive months)
    - Suffered a hardship (that affects his or her ability to purchase health insurance coverage)
    - Didn't have access to affordable coverage (cost of available coverage greater than 8.13% of household income)
    - Were incarcerated (unless pending disposition of charges)
    - Weren't lawfully present in the U.S.
    - Had your health insurance cancelled and the Marketplace plans weren't affordable

3. You May Pay a Fee (Shared Responsibility Payment)

- You may pay a fee when you file your 2015 federal tax return in 2016 (and thereafter)
    - If you don't have minimum essential coverage, and
    - Don't qualify for an exemption
- Paying the fee doesn't provide health coverage

How much is the fee?

- If you don't have health insurance in 2016, you'll pay the higher of these two amounts:
  - 2.5% of your yearly household income (Only the amount of income above the tax filing threshold, about $10,150 for an individual in 2014, is used to calculate the penalty)
    - The maximum penalty is the national average premium for a Bronze plan
  - $695 per person ($347.50 per child under 18)
    - The maximum penalty per family using this method is $2,085
- The penalty for noncompliance can't exceed the national average premium for a Bronze level Marketplace QHP (for the relevant family size)
- After 2016, the amounts increase based on the cost of living

When You Can Enroll in Coverage

- During the Open Enrollment Period (OEP)
  - For coverage in 2017 and 2018, OEP will be November 1 of the previews year and run through January 31 of the coverage year
  - For coverage in 2019 and beyond, open enrollment will begin on November 1 and end on December 15 of the preceding year
- During a Special Enrollment Period (SEP), if eligible
- Once per month if member of federally recognized Indian tribe or Alaska native shareholder
- Anytime you're eligible for Medicaid or the Children's Health Insurance Program

How to Enroll During a Special Enrollment Period for a Qualifying Life Event

- If you have a qualifying life event, you can update your information
  - Online at <u>HealthCare.gov</u>
    - Log into your account and click on Report a life change
  - By phone
    - Call the Marketplace Call Center at 1-800-318-2596
    - TTY 1-855-889-4325

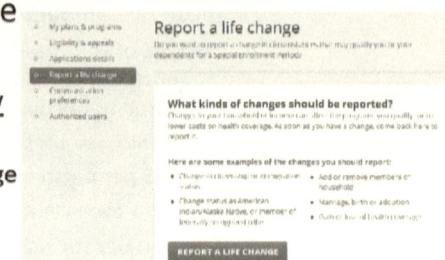

How the Federally-facilitated and State-Partnership Marketplaces Work

Create an account

Go to HealthCare.gov/get-coverage and provide some basic information. Then choose a password and security questions for added protection.

Apply

Next you'll enter information about you and your family, including your income, household size, other coverage you're eligible for, and more.

Pick a plan

Next you'll see all the plans and programs you're eligible for. You can compare qualified health plans side-by-side.

You'll also see if you can get lower costs on monthly premiums and other savings based on your income.

Enroll

Choose a plan that meets your needs, enroll, and pay your first premium.

You're covered!

May apply or change plan during Special Enrollment Period due to certain qualifying events.

Premium Payment

- You must pay the first month's premium directly to your insurance company by the insurer's deadline
- You must pay the premium each month or you could lose coverage
- Issuers must accept at least these payment methods
  - Paper check
  - Cashier's check
  - Money order
  - Electronic fund transfer (EFT)
  - Pre-paid debit card
- Some issuers may also accept online, credit card, or debit card payments (check with the plan)

Marketplace Appeals

- If you don't agree with a decision made by a Health Insurance Marketplace, you may be able to file an appeal.
- You can appeal the following kinds of Marketplace decisions
  - Whether you're eligible to buy a Marketplace plan
  - Whether you can enroll in a Marketplace plan outside the regular Open Enrollment Period
  - Whether you're eligible for lower costs based on their income
  - The amount of savings you're eligible for
  - Whether you're eligible for Medicaid or the Children's Health Insurance Program (CHIP)
  - Whether you're eligible for an exemption from the individual responsibility requirement (fee)

Enrollment Assistance

- Help is available in the Marketplace
  - Marketplace Call Center
  - Marketplace-approved in-person help is available
- Use the Find Local Help tool at Localhelp.HealthCare.gov/
- Language assistance is available through interpreters, Call Center support, and print and web resources
- Help is available to complete application
  - Job aids in 33 languages

Marketplace Call Center

- Services consumers in Federally-facilitated and State-Partnership Marketplaces
  - 1-800-318-2596 (TTY 1-855-889-4325)
- Customer service representatives available 24/7
- Help with eligibility, enrollment, and referrals
- Assistance in English and Spanish
  - Oral interpretations for 240+ additional languages
- State-based Marketplaces have own Call Centers

Small Business Health Options Program (SHOP) Call Center

- For questions about SHOP
  - 1-800-706-7893 (TTY 711)
- Customer service representatives available Monday – Friday from 9 a.m. to 7 p.m. ET

Marketplaces and People with Medicare

- Medicare isn't part of a Marketplace
- If you have Medicare, you don't need to do anything related to the Marketplaces
  - Your benefits don't change because of the Marketplaces
  - It's illegal to sell you a Marketplace plan
    - Except an employer through the Small Business Health Options Program (SHOP) if you're an active worker or dependent of an active worker
      - The SHOP employer coverage may pay first
      - No late enrollment penalty if you delay Medicare
      - Doesn't include COBRA coverage

From Coverage to Care

Written materials available in English, Spanish, Korean, Chinese, Vietnamese, Haitian, Creole, Arabic, and Russian. There is also a Tribal version.

Marketplace.cms.gov/technical-assistance-resources/c2c.html#Resources

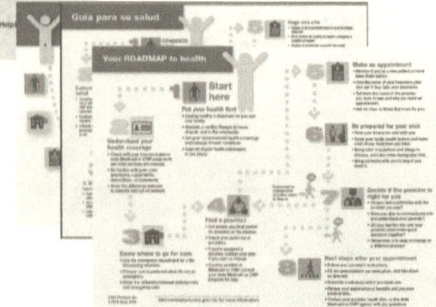

Videos in English and Spanish

March 2016   Marketplace 101   33

Marketplace.cms.gov

March 2016   Marketplace 101   34

Small Business Health Options Program (SHOP) Call Center

- For questions about SHOP
  - 1-800-706-7893 (TTY 711)
- Customer service representatives available Monday – Friday from 9 a.m. to 7 p.m. ET

Marketplaces and People with Medicare

- Medicare isn't part of a Marketplace
- If you have Medicare, you don't need to do anything related to the Marketplaces
  - Your benefits don't change because of the Marketplaces
  - It's illegal to sell you a Marketplace plan
    - Except an employer through the Small Business Health Options Program (SHOP) if you're an active worker or dependent of an active worker
      - The SHOP employer coverage may pay first
      - No late enrollment penalty if you delay Medicare
      - Doesn't include COBRA coverage

From Coverage to Care

Written materials available in English, Spanish, Korean, Chinese, Vietnamese, Haitian, Creole, Arabic, and Russian. There is also a Tribal version.

Marketplace.cms.gov/technical-assistance-resources/c2c.html#Resources

Videos in English and Spanish

Marketplace.cms.gov

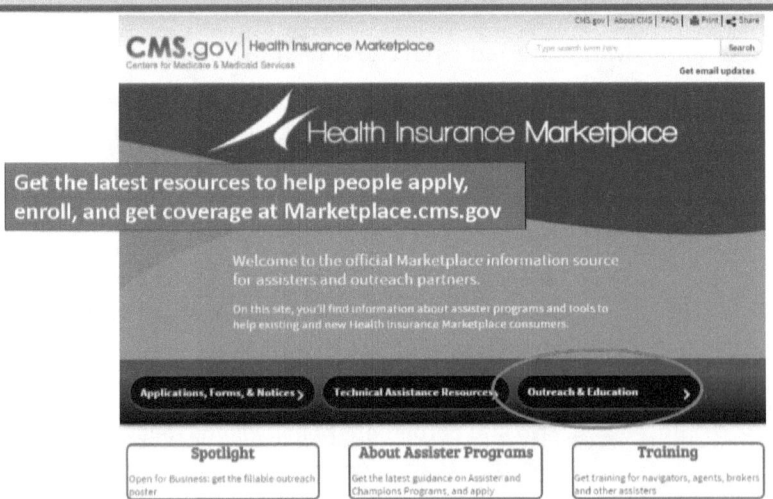

Want More Information about the Marketplace?

- Twitter@HealthCareGov
- Facebook.com/Healthcare.gov?_rdr=p
- YouTube.com/playlist?list=PLaV7m2-zFKpgZDNCz7rZ3Xx7q2cDmpAm7
- Sign up to get email and text alerts at HealthCare.gov/subscribe
  - CuidadoDeSalud.gov for Spanish
- Updates and resources for organizations are available at Marketplace.cms.gov

Key Points to Remember

- A Marketplace is a way for qualified individuals and families to find and buy health insurance
  - You may enroll or change plans during a Special Enrollment Period if you have certain qualifying life events
- Eligible small employers can cover their employees through the SHOP
- States have flexibility to establish their own Marketplace
- Individuals and families may be eligible for lower costs on their monthly premiums and out-of-pocket costs
- There is help available
- If a you don't agree with a decision made by a Marketplace, you may be able to file an appeal

Health Insurance Marketplace:
10 Things to Tell Your Patients

1. If you don't already have health coverage, the Health Insurance Marketplace is a way to find and buy health coverage that fits your budget and meets your needs.

2. You can enroll during Open Enrollment or during a Special Enrollment Period if you qualify because of a life change. Check **HealthCare.gov** each fall for Open Enrollment dates.

3. Each state has a Marketplace, run either by the state, through a state-federal partnership, or by the federal government.

4. With one simple application, you can find out if you might be eligible for help paying for Marketplace coverage or for programs like Medicaid or the Children's Health Insurance Program (CHIP).

5. You can apply online at **HealthCare.gov**, by phone, by mail, or in-person with the help of a trained assister or navigator.

6. Each health plan generally will offer comprehensive coverage, including a core set of essential health benefits like doctor visits, preventive care, maternity care, hospitalization, prescription drugs, and more.

7. No matter where you live, the Marketplace will offer plans from private companies and you'll be able to compare your health coverage options based on price, benefits, quality, and other features important to you before you make a choice.

8. Health insurance companies selling plans through the Marketplace can't deny you coverage or charge you more due to pre-existing health conditions, and they can't charge women and men different premiums based on their sex.

9. Once you're covered through the Marketplace, it's important to update information at **HealthCare.gov** if your situation or income changes, and return each year to compare available plans, then re-enroll or switch.

10. For more information, visit **HealthCare.gov**. Or, call the Marketplace Call Center at **1-800-318-2596**, 24 hours a day, 7 days a week. TTY users should call **1-855-889-4325**.

Health Insurance Marketplace

CMS Product No. 11717-P
Revised July 2015

No Health Coverage? Find Out if You'll Owe a Fee

If you didn't qualify for Medicaid or Children's Health Insurance Program (CHIP) coverage, and you aren't eligible for lower costs through the Health Insurance Marketplace, you still have options that could help.

If you can't afford health coverage, you're not required to buy it. You can apply for an exemption so you won't have to pay a fee for going without coverage. You don't need to apply if you live in a state that didn't expand Medicaid and your Marketplace eligibility notice says you have an exemption.

For more information:

- Visit HealthCare.gov/exemptions
- Visit findahealthcenter.hrsa.gov to locate a community health center near you
- Visit HealthCare.gov/lower-costs/ to see if you qualify for lower costs on health insurance coverage

Health Insurance Marketplace

CMS Product No. 11796
Revised September 2015

Medicare & the Health Insurance Marketplace

The Health Insurance Marketplace, a key part of the Affordable Care Act, is a way for individuals, families, and employees of small businesses to get health coverage.

If I have Medicare, do I need to do anything?

No. Medicare isn't part of the Marketplace. If you have Medicare, you're covered and don't need to do anything about the Marketplace.

The Marketplace doesn't affect your Medicare choices or benefits. No matter how you get Medicare, whether through Original Medicare or a Medicare Advantage Plan (like an HMO or PPO), you don't have to make any changes.

Note: The Marketplace doesn't offer Medicare Supplement Insurance (Medigap) policies or Medicare drug plans (Part D).

Does Medicare coverage meet the Affordable Care Act's requirement that all Americans have health insurance?

If you have Medicare Part A (Hospital Insurance), you're considered covered and won't need a Marketplace plan. Having Medicare Part B (Medical Insurance) alone doesn't meet this requirement.

Can I get a Marketplace plan in addition to Medicare?

No. It's against the law for someone who knows that you have Medicare to sell you a Marketplace plan. This is true even if you have only Part A or only Part B.

If you want coverage designed to supplement Medicare, visit Medicare.gov to learn more about Medigap policies. You can also visit **Medicare.gov** to learn more about other Medicare options, like Medicare Advantage Plans.

Can I choose Marketplace coverage instead of Medicare?

Generally, no. As noted above, it's against the law for someone who knows you have Medicare to sell you a Marketplace plan. However, there are some situations where you can choose Marketplace coverage instead of Medicare:

- You can choose Marketplace coverage if you're eligible for Medicare but haven't enrolled in it (because you would have to pay a premium, or because you're not collecting Social Security benefits).
- If you're paying a premium for Part A, you can drop your Part A and Part B coverage and get a Marketplace plan.

Note: If you get premium-free Part A, you can't drop Medicare without also dropping your retiree or disability benefits (Social Security or Railroad Retirement Board). You'll also have to pay back all retirement or disability benefits you've received and all costs paid by Medicare for your health care claims.

Before making either of these choices, there are two important points to consider:

- If you enroll in Medicare after your Initial Enrollment Period ends, you may have to pay a late enrollment penalty for as long as you have Medicare.
- Generally, you can enroll in Medicare only during the Medicare General Enrollment Period (from January 1– March 31). Your coverage won't begin until July of that year.

What if I become eligible for Medicare after I join a Marketplace plan?

You can get a Marketplace plan to cover you before your Medicare begins. You can then cancel the Marketplace plan once your Medicare coverage starts.

Once you're eligible for Medicare, you'll have an Initial Enrollment Period to sign up. For most people, the Initial Enrollment Period for Medicare starts 3 months before their 65th birthday and ends 3 months after their 65th birthday.

In most cases, it's to your advantage to sign up when you're first eligible because:

- Once you're eligible for Medicare, you won't be able to get lower costs for a Marketplace plan based on your income.
- If you enroll in Medicare after your Initial Enrollment Period ends, you may have to pay a late enrollment penalty for as long as you have Medicare.

Note: You can keep your Marketplace plan after your Medicare coverage starts. However, once your Part A coverage starts, any tax credits and reduced cost-sharing you get through the Marketplace will stop.

If I have Medicare, can I get health coverage from an employer through the SHOP Marketplace?

Yes. Coverage from an employer through the SHOP Marketplace is treated the same as coverage from an employer group health plan. If you're getting health coverage from an employer through the SHOP Marketplace based on you or your spouse's current employment, Medicare Secondary Payer rules apply. Visit **Medicare.gov** to learn more about how Medicare works with other insurance.

If I'm getting health coverage from an employer through the SHOP Marketplace, can I delay enrollment in Part B without a penalty?

Yes. You can delay enrollment if you're getting health coverage from an employer through the SHOP Marketplace based on you or your spouse's current employment. You have a Special Enrollment Period to sign up for Part B without penalty:

- Any time you're still covered by the group health plan based on you or your spouse's current employment.
- During the 8-month period that begins the month after the employment ends or the coverage ends, whichever happens first.

If you don't sign up during this Special Enrollment Period:

- You may have to pay a late enrollment penalty.
- You can only enroll during the General Enrollment Period which occurs each year from January – March with coverage beginning July 1.

I have End-Stage Renal Disease (ESRD), but I haven't signed up for Medicare. Can I get a Marketplace plan?

Yes. People with ESRD aren't required to sign up for Medicare. If you have ESRD and don't have either Medicare Part A or Part B, you can get a Marketplace plan. You may also be eligible for tax credits and reduced cost-sharing through the Marketplace.

I have Medicare coverage due to ESRD. Can I drop my Medicare coverage and choose a Marketplace plan?

Generally, no. Once you apply for Medicare, your Medicare coverage will end one year after you stop getting regular dialysis or 36 months after a successful kidney transplant. However, you may withdraw your original Medicare application. You would have to repay all costs covered by Medicare, pay any outstanding balances, and refund any benefits you got from Social Security or the Railroad Retirement Board. Once you've made all of the repayments, the withdrawal will be processed as though you never had Medicare at all.

Can I get a stand-alone dental plan through the Marketplace?

In most cases, no. If the Marketplace in your state is run by the federal government, you won't be able buy a stand-alone dental plan. If your state is running its own Marketplace, you may be able to purchase a stand-alone dental plan, if one's available.

Is prescription drug coverage through the Marketplace considered creditable prescription drug coverage for Medicare Part D?

While prescription drug coverage is an essential health benefit, prescription drug coverage in a Marketplace or SHOP plan isn't required to be at least as good as Medicare Part D coverage (creditable). However, all private insurers offering prescription drug coverage, including Marketplace and SHOP plans, are required to determine if their prescription drug coverage is creditable each year and let you know in writing. Visit **Medicare.gov** for more information about creditable coverage.

How can I get help paying for my Medicare costs?

- If you need help with your Part A and B costs, you can apply for a Medicare Savings Program. Call your state Medical Assistance (Medicaid) office. To get their phone number, visit **Medicare.gov/contacts**, or call 1-800-MEDICARE (1-800-633-4227). TTY users should call 1-877-486-2048.
- If you need Extra Help to pay for Medicare prescription drug costs, visit **socialsecurity.gov/i1020**, or call Social Security at 1-800-772-1213. TTY users should call 1-800-325-0778.

Where can I get more information?

- To learn more about Medicare enrollment, coverage, and plan choices, visit **Medicare.gov**, or call 1-800-MEDICARE.
- If you have family and friends who don't have health coverage, or if they want to explore health plan options, tell them to visit **HealthCare.gov**.

CMS Product No. 11694
Revised September 2014

How to Apply for Coverage

Use one of these ways to apply for and enroll in Marketplace coverage:

1. Online:
Visit HealthCare.gov/get-coverage, and select your state. Be sure to write down your email address and a hint to remember your password in case you need them later. Store them in a safe place.

Email address: _____

Password hint: _____

2. By phone:
Call the Marketplace Call Center at **1-800-318-2596.** TTY users should call **1-855-889-4325.**

3. With in-person help:
Visit Localhelp.HealthCare.gov for free in-person help in your community.

When you apply, you'll be asked if anyone on your application is incarcerated. Read this statement carefully before you answer. You'll need to add more information if you (or someone else on your application) is pending disposition of charges.

CMS Product No. 11959
December 2015

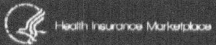

Health Insurance Marketplace

UNDERSTANDING THE HEALTH INSURANCE MARKETPLACE

IF YOU'RE INCARCERATED

Read this card for more information on Marketplace health coverage if you're currently incarcerated (held involuntarily in a prison, jail, detention center, or police lock-up) or were recently released from incarceration.

If You're Currently Incarcerated

You aren't eligible for certain programs in the Marketplace, even if you'll be released soon. You can enroll in Marketplace coverage after you're released.

Because you're not eligible to enroll in coverage while incarcerated, you won't have to pay the fee that others without health coverage have to pay.

If You Haven't Been Convicted

If you're detained in jail or prison, but haven't been convicted of charges, you can enroll in Marketplace coverage, if you're eligible. See "How to Apply for Coverage."

If you're eligible, you'll need to apply for and enroll in coverage, or you may owe a fee, unless you qualify for an exemption. For more information, visit HealthCare.gov/fees/fee-for-not-being-covered.

If You were Recently Released from Incarceration

You have a 60-day Special Enrollment Period to sign up for Marketplace coverage. During this time, you can enroll in a plan, even if it's outside of the Marketplace Open Enrollment Period. See "How to Apply for Coverage."

If you don't apply for and enroll in coverage during your 60-day Special Enrollment Period, you won't be able to get Marketplace coverage until the next Marketplace Open Enrollment Period, unless you qualify for a different Special Enrollment Period. For more information, visit HealthCare.gov/coverage-outside-open-enrollment/special-enrollment-period.

If you're eligible you'll need to apply for and enroll in coverage, or you may owe a fee, unless you qualify for an exemption. For more information, visit HealthCare.gov/fees/fee-for-not-being-covered.

College students have several choices for health coverage.

A student health plan

If you're covered by your school's student health plan, in most cases, you're considered covered under the Affordable Care Act. You won't have to pay the fee that people without coverage must generally pay. Check with your student health plan to see if it qualifies as coverage under the health care law.

A Marketplace health plan

You can choose to buy a health plan through the Health Insurance Marketplace. Most people qualify for financial help to lower premium costs. Visit HealthCare.gov to apply and find out if you can get lower costs for health coverage.

Coverage on a parent's plan

You may be able to stay on or get added to your parent's health plan until you turn 26.

Catastrophic health plans

If you're under 30, you can buy a catastrophic health plan to protect yourself from the high costs of an accident or serious illness. These plans usually have lower monthly premiums, but high deductibles. You pay for most of your care yourself, up to a certain amount. After that, the insurance company pays its share for covered services.

Medicaid coverage

Medicaid is a combined state and federal program that provides coverage to people with limited income. When you apply for coverage at HealthCare.gov, you'll find out if you qualify for coverage through Medicaid.

What if I don't have health coverage?

If you can afford health insurance, but you don't have it, you may have to pay a fee with your income tax return. There's no special student exemption. However, you won't have to pay the fee if you have a limited income and you don't have to file a federal tax return.

For more information, visit HealthCare.gov, or call the Marketplace Call Center at 1-800-318-2596. TTY users should call 1-855-889-4325.

Dates & deadlines for 2016 health insurance

Open Enrollment for 2016 health coverage ended January 31, 2016.

If you didn't enroll by January 31, 2016, you can't enroll in a health insurance plan for 2016 unless you qualify for a Special Enrollment Period. *(Special Enrollment Period- A time outside of the open enrollment period during which you and your family have a right to sign up for health coverage. In the Marketplace, you qualify for a special enrollment period 60 days following certain life events that involve a change in family status (for example, marriage or birth of a child) or loss of other health coverage. Job-based plans must provide a special enrollment period of 30 days.)*

Medicaid & Children's Health Insurance Program (CHIP) – apply any time

There's no limited enrollment period for Medicaid or CHIP. You can apply any time. To see if you may qualify and next steps, visit this https://www.healthcare.gov/screener/ and select the second button, titled "See if you may qualify for Medicaid or CHIP."

Next open enrollment

The Open Enrollment Period for 2017 is November 1, 2016 — January 31, 2017. Sign up for emails to get deadline reminders and other important information.

Questions? Call 24 Hours (TTY: 1-855-889-4325)

Health Insurance MarketplaceTips

1. The Health Insurance Marketplace is for people who don't have health coverage

a. If you don't have health insurance through a job, Medicare, Medicaid, CHIP, or another source that provides qualifying coverage, the Marketplace can help you get covered.

b. If you have job-based insurance: You can buy a plan through the Marketplace, but you'll pay full price unless your employer's insurance doesn't meet certain standards. Most job-based plans do meet the standards.

c. If you have Medicare: You can't switch to Marketplace insurance, supplement your coverage with a Marketplace plan, or buy a Marketplace dental plan. Learn about Medicare and the Marketplace.

2. What you pay for insurance depends on your income – and you'll probably save

a. Your savings depend on your estimate of your **expected income for 2016,** not your income for 2015. This year, about 8 in 10 of the uninsured who are eligible for Marketplace coverage qualify for financial assistance to lower the cost of their monthly premiums. Get a quick idea if your expected income is in the range to save.

3. Based on the income estimate you put on your application, we'll tell you if you qualify for one of these:
   a. A health insurance plan with savings
      i. Most people who apply qualify for a premium tax credit that lowers their monthly insurance bill. Some also save on out of pocket costs like deductibles and copayments.
      ii. The plans are offered by private insurance companies with a range of prices and features. All plans cover:

   b. Essential health Benefits

      i. Pre-existing conditions, including pregnancy

      ii. Preventive care

      iii. You can add dental to a health plan, but you don't have to. You can't buy a dental plan unless you enroll in a health plan.
   c. Medicaid and the Children's Health Insurance Program (CHIP)
      i. Medicaid and CHIP provide free or low-cost coverage to millions of people and

families with limited income, disabilities, and some other situations.

    ii. Many states are expanding Medicaid to cover all households below certain incomes. See if your state is expanding and if your income is in range to qualify.

    iii. Your children may qualify for CHIP even if you don't qualify for Medicaid.

4. **You can apply for coverage four ways**

    a. You can apply for health insurance any way that works for you:

        i. Online

        ii. By phone

        iii. With in-person help

        iv. With a paper application

        v. **If you don't have health insurance, you may have to pay a fee**

5. Most people must have qualifying health coverage or pay a fee with their 2016 Federal taxes.

6. If you don't have coverage in 2016, you'll pay a penalty of either 2.5% of your income, or $695 per

adult ($347.50 per child) — whichever is higher.
Learn about the fee.

7. In some cases, you might qualify for an exemption
from the requirement to have health insurance.

Dental Coverage In The Marketplace

In the Health Insurance Marketplace, you can get dental coverage
two ways:

1. As part of a health plan
2. By itself through a separate, stand-alone dental
plan.

Note: You can buy a dental plan through the Federal Marketplace
only when you enroll in a health plan. Some states that run their
own Marketplaces allow you to buy a dental plan without also
buying a health plan.

Dental Coverage is Available Two Ways:

- Health plans that include dental coverage. In the
Marketplace, dental coverage is included in some health
plans. You can see which plans include dental coverage
when you compare them.
  - If a health plan includes dental coverage, you'll pay
one monthly premium for everything. The premium
shown for the plan includes both health and dental
coverage.
- Separate, stand-alone dental plans. In some cases
separate, stand-alone plans are offered.
  - You may want this if the health coverage you
choose does not include dental coverage, or if you
want different dental coverage.
  - If you choose a separate dental plan, you'll pay a
separate, additional premium.

Adult and Child Dental Insurance in the Marketplace

Under the health care law, dental insurance is treated differently for adults and children 18 and under.

Dental Coverage for Children:

Is an essential health benefit. This means if you're getting coverage for someone 18 or younger, dental coverage must be available as part of a health plan or as a stand-alone plan. While it must be available to you, you do not have to buy it.

This is not the case for adults:

Insurers do not have to offer adult dental coverage. Under the health care law, most people must have health coverage or pay a penalty. But this is not true for dental coverage. You do not need to have dental coverage, even for children, to avoid the penalty.

How To Enroll In The S.H.O.P. Marketplace

You apply for and enroll in S.H.O.P. coverage for employees of your small business directly through an agent, broker, or insurance company.

You can enroll in S.H.O.P. throughout the year. The deadline to enroll is always the 15th of the month for coverage to be effective the 1st of the following month.

IMPORTANT FACTS ABOUT S.H.O.P. COVERAGE FOR YOUR EMPLOYEES

How to Enroll in the SHOP Marketplace for Employees

The online Small Business Health Options Program (SHOP) Marketplace is now open for employers with 100 or fewer employees. If you have SHOP Marketplace coverage, check with your employer to find out when it's time to renew or change your coverage on **HealthCare.gov**.

If your employer is in a state that isn't running its own SHOP Marketplace, you'll use HealthCare.gov to enroll. Visit **HealthCare.gov/small-businesses/employees** and select the state where your employer's primary address is located. Then, follow the steps below.

If your employer is in a state that's running its own SHOP Marketplace, follow your state's application process. To find the SHOP Marketplace in your state, visit **HealthCare.gov/small-businesses/employees** and select your state from the drop down menu.

Create a HealthCare.gov account

If your employer is offering coverage through the SHOP Marketplace, you may get an email notice with a participation code. You'll use this information to view and respond to your employer's coverage offer. If you don't have an email address, your employer will get this information to you.

- Select **SEE HOW TO ACCEPT OR DECLINE**. On this page you'll learn how to accept or decline your employer's SHOP Marketplace coverage offer. To create a HealthCare.gov account, select this link: **If you don't have a HealthCare.gov account, create one**.
  - If you already have a HealthCare.gov account you created previously to apply for individual and family coverage, log into the same account to access the SHOP Marketplace. Skip to **Confirm eligibility** below to continue with these steps.

  Note: If you think your employer is offering SHOP Marketplace coverage and you haven't gotten a notice with your participation code, contact your employer, not the SHOP Marketplace. Your employer can provide your participation code. **There's nothing you can do here until you get the participation code.**

■ **Enter your employee information.** On the **Create an account** page, you'll enter your name, email address, preferred password, and set up a few security questions. These questions will be helpful in case you forget your username and/or password and have trouble logging in.

Note: The create an account page is for all Marketplace users – individuals and families, small businesses, and small business employees.

Select **CREATE ACCOUNT**. Follow the instructions on the screen to verify your email address and start using the SHOP Marketplace.

Confirm eligibility

■ **Log into your HealthCare.gov account.** Enter your username and password, review the **Terms & Conditions**, and then select **I ACCEPT**.

■ **Select the employee application.** On the **WELCOME TO THE MARKETPLACE** page, select **VISIT EMPLOYEE MARKETPLACE**.

■ **Enter the SHOP participation code.** On the **My employer** page, enter the participation code given to you by your employer, and your Social Security Number (SSN) or an alternative number to your SSN given to you by your employer. You should do this even if you don't want coverage now, then select **VERIFY**. Select **Yes** to add the employer to your account.

Review coverage offer

On the **My employer page**, select **Begin** in the **Action** field to start reviewing your employer's coverage offer.

■ **Accept or decline your employer's coverage offer.** You can return and change your response after viewing health plans.

If you accept the coverage offer, enter employee details, like mailing address and other contact information.

• **Add dependents.** If your employer is offering dependent coverage, select **ADD DEPENDENT(S)**.

• **Sign the enrollment application.** Enter your name in the box to sign the application, then select **SAVE AND CONTINUE**.

If you decline the coverage offer, select the reason from the drop down menu.

- **Verify your decision to decline coverage.** Read and agree with the statements.

- **Sign the enrollment application.** Enter your name in the box to sign the application, then select **SUBMIT**. **If you're declining coverage, no further action is required.**

Select plan(s)

- **Review employer's health coverage.** The plan(s) you'll see are based on your employer's primary business address. Select **View plan details** to see plan details, like copayments, laboratory and outpatient services, medical devices, emergency care, and inpatient hospital services. If your employer is offering you a choice of plans, you'll see a list of plans to compare.

  - **Compare plans**. If you have multiple plans listed, you can select up to 3 plans to compare side-by-side. Select the **Compare** checkbox for each plan you want to compare. Then, select **Compare plans**.

  - **Sort plans**. Select **Sort by** on the drop down menu to see your options.

  - **Filter plans**. You can use the menu listing on the left side of the the page to narrow your plan search based on certain criteria.

- **Select one health plan and one dental plan (if offered).** To choose plan(s) for you and your dependents, click **Select** next to the health plan information. Then, select **CONTINUE**.

Complete enrollment

- **Review plan selection(s) and cost.** Read the summary of your health and dental plan (if offered).

- **Confirm plan choice(s).** Select **CONFIRM** to submit your application.

- **Get a confirmation.** You'll get a confirmation letting you know that your application is complete. It includes a confirmation number that you should keep for your records.

- **View enrollment.** Select **Return to My enrollment** to view the details of your enrollment.

- **Don't want to buy coverage?** Select **WAIVE**.
  - On the page that says **I'm declining this coverage offer**, select the health coverage you currently have or will have once your employer's coverage is effective. Then, select **WAIVE**.

If you have questions about the SHOP Marketplace or need help with the employee application, contact the SHOP Call Center at 1-800-706-7893, Monday through Friday from 9 AM – 7 PM ET. TTY users should call 711 to reach a call center representative.

For more information about the SHOP Marketplace, visit **HealthCare.gov/small-businesses.**

SHOP Marketplace
Health Insurance for Small Businesses

CMS Product No. 11877
Revised September 2015

Patient Protection And Affordable Care Act:

Adds many protections related to employment-based group health plans for you and your family. These include:

Additional protections that may apply to your plan include the requirement to provide coverage for certain preventive services (such as blood pressure, diabetes and cholesterol tests, regular well-baby and well-child visits, routine vaccinations and many cancer screenings) without cost-sharing, and coverage of emergency services in an emergency department of a hospital outside your plan's network without prior approval from your health plan.

The Affordable Care Act also provides coverage options that allow you to maintain health coverage for you and your family. This page provides information on the Affordable Care Act to help you consider your options and make informed decisions, along with contact information if you have further questions.

Employers must provide notice to employees of coverage options. No later than November 1, 2015, employers will be providing these notices to current employees and to new hires within 14 days. If your employer offers a health plan to some or all employees, you will receive this notice. If your employer does not offer a health plan, you will receive this notice.

Option 1: Your Employer Plan

The Affordable Care Act adds numerous protections related to

employment-based group health plans. These include:

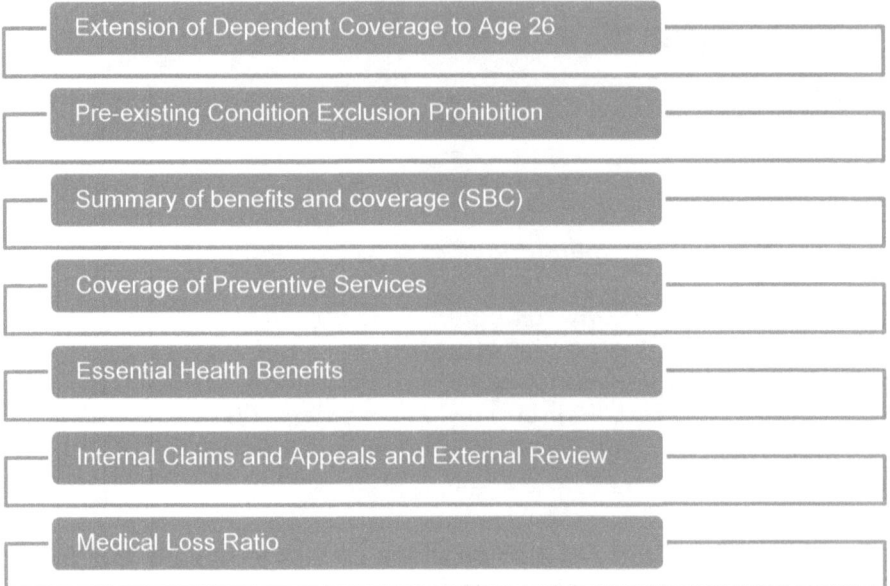

Extension of Dependent Coverage to Age 26

Pre-existing Condition Exclusion Prohibition

Summary of benefits and coverage (SBC)

Coverage of Preventive Services

Essential Health Benefits

Internal Claims and Appeals and External Review

Medical Loss Ratio

The Affordable Care Act prohibits employers from retaliating
against employees who report violations of the Act's health
insurance reforms, found in Title I of the Affordable Care Act. For
more information, visit www.whistleblowers.gov. For a full list of
Affordable Care Act provisions, visit
www.dol.gov/ebsa/healthreform/.

Option 2 – The Health Insurance Marketplace

Under the Affordable Care Act, in addition to health coverage through an employment-based group health plan, there will be a new way to get health coverage – the new Health Insurance Marketplace (the Marketplace).

The Marketplace will offer health insurance (called **qualified health plans**) that include *comprehensive coverage*, from doctors and medications to hospital visits.

> **Qualified health plans in the Marketplace will present their price and benefit information in simple terms so that you can make apples-to-apples comparisons. Starting in October 2013, you will be able to get information about all of the plans available in your area and enroll.**

For more information about obtaining coverage through the Marketplace, visit www.healthcare.gov, contact EBSA electronically at www.askebsa.dol.gov, or call the HealthCare.gov Help Line at 1-800-318-2596.

Oklahoma Health Care

Medical Programs Contact:

Oklahoma State Department of Health
1000 NE 10th
Oklahoma City, OK 73117
Local: (405) 271-5600
Toll-Free: (800) 522-0203

Oklahoma Department of Human Services
http://www.okhca.org/
Address:444 S. Houston Tulsa, OK 74127
Phone: (918) 581-2401 or 1-800-734-7516
Fax: (918) 581-2114

Sooner Care (Oklahoma Medicaid)
Sooner Care Helpline at 1-800-987-7767.

A health coverage program jointly funded by the Federal and State government. This program helps pay some or all medical bills for many people who cannot afford them.

You can use a form to apply for SoonerCare health insurance for yourself and everyone in your immediate family who lives with you. You may download the English or Spanish application, fill it out and mail it in. If you need help filling out the form, call the

WHAT ABOUT MEDICARE?
MEDICARE IS DIFFERENT FROM SOONERCARE (OKLAHOMA MEDICAID). MEDICARE IS A FEDERAL HEALTH INSURANCE PROGRAM ADMINISTERED BY THE CENTERS FOR MEDICARE & MEDICAID SERVICES (CMS). MEDICARE PROVIDES COVERAGE MOSTLY TO INDIVIDUALS AGE 65 OR OLDER AND SOME PEOPLE WITH DISABILITIES.

IF YOU ARE ON MEDICARE AND YOU QUALIFY FOR SOONERCARE, MOST OF YOUR HEALTH CARE COSTS ARE COVERED. IF YOU HAVE LOW-INCOME AND LIMITED ASSETS, SOONERCARE MAY HELP PAY

SOME OR ALL OF MEDICARE PREMIUMS AND COST-SHARING EXPENSES.

Sooner care Programs

InSure Oklahoma

Individuals who are employed, self-employed, temporarily unemployed or working disabled may apply online for Insure Oklahoma.

- What services are paid?
  Covered health care services may include doctor visits, hospitalization and prescriptions.

- What does it cost?
  There is no cost for those who meet the income guidelines; however, co-pays may apply to some services.

College Students (Between Ages 19 and 22)

To qualify for SoonerCare, a person must: Reside in Oklahoma; Be a U.S. citizen or qualified alien (most immigrants who arrived after August 22, 1996 are barred from the program for five years); Meet financial income and resources standards in certain categories.

American Indians

Health Service, tribal and Urban Indian Health programs.

Child Health

Early and Periodic Screening, Diagnosis and Treatment, is a preventive health care package for children age 20 or younger enrolled in Oklahoma Medicaid.

Long-Term Care Services

Health care providing Long-Term Care and support in home and community-based settings, in nursing homes, in small and large residential care facilities or group homes, and in the workplace. This includes Living Choice, PACE, Focus On Excellence, Oklahoma Long-Term Care Partnership, Certified Nurse Aide Training program and more.

Applying for Long-Term Care.
- Age 65 or over
- Blind (any age)
- Disabled adults
- Disabled children who do not qualify for Social Security Income because of their parents income and/or resources (TEFRA)
- Individuals who reside in nursing homes, yet qualify for SoonerCare
- Individuals with Medicare coverage that need assistance to pay premiums, coinsurance and/or deductibles
- Home and community-based waiver populations
- Children in the custody of OKDHS
- Individuals who receive treatment for Tuberculosis (TB). Benefits through SoonerCare are limited to TB drugs and TB clinic visits and only if the individual has active TB. These Benefits are for a limited amount of time only

Oklahoma Cares
Women with Breast and/or Cervical Cancer.
Once you have been screened and found to be in need of further diagnosis and/or treatment for breast or cervical cancer, you or your screener can call the Oklahoma State Department of Health.

Pregnancy Services
Services designed to ensure that every qualified pregnant woman has access to medical care, with the goal of lowering Oklahoma's infant mortality rate and improving maternal and infant health.

SoonerCare Health Management Program-chronic Disease
An innovative and comprehensive approach to chronic disease management.

SoonerCare Supplemental –Co-Insurance
A plan that pays the coinsurance and deductible and provides medical Benefits that supplement those services covered by Medicare.

SoonerCare Traditional - Institutionalized

A comprehensive medical benefit plan that purchases Benefits for members as they receive a service.

SoonerCare Traditional provides coverage for members **who qualify for Medicaid and are institutionalized, in State or tribal custody or enrolled under a Home and Community-Based Waiver.** The member accesses services from contracted providers, and the OHCA pays the provider on a fee-for-service basis.

SoonerPlan –Family Plaming

A benefit plan covering limited services related to family planning, to women and men ages 19 and older, in an effort to reduce unwanted pregnancies.

SoonerRide

provides free non-emergency transportation to and from SoonerCare covered appointments.

SoonerCare Choice-Medical Home Provider

Primary Care Case Management program in which each member has a medical home. The medical home provider will coordinate all health care services to qualifying Oklahomans.

TEFRA (Tax Equity And Fiscal Responsibility Act Of 1982),

Care for **Children with Disabilities allows** members under age 19 with special health care needs or disabilities to be cared for at home instead of in an institution.

Children's Health Coverage Programs In Oklahoma

Call 1-877 KIDS NOW (1-877-543-7669)

Medicaid and CHIP

Provide no cost or low-cost health coverage for eligible children in Oklahoma. *Even if your children have been turned down in the past or you do not know if they qualify, you may be able to get health coverage for them now.*

Medicaid and CHIP provide health coverage for children so that they can get routine check-ups, immunizations and dental care to keep them healthy. They can also get doctor visits, prescription medications and hospital care when they're sick, and much more.

Dental Care

Your child needs to have Medicaid or CHIP coverage in order to get dental Benefits. Once your child has coverage through Medicaid or CHIP, he or she can get dental care.

Domestic Violence Survivor
Survivor Witness Coordinator
Contact Information by County:

Adair: 220 W. Division St.,
Stillwell, 74960
(918)696-7150

Alfalfa: 300 S. Grand,
Cherokee, 73728
(580)256-8616

Atoka: 200 E. Court St.,
Atoka, 74525
(580)924-4421

Beaver: 111
W. 2nd St., Beaver, 73932
(580)338-3604

Beckham: 301 E. Main,
Sayre, 73662
(580)928-2054

Blaine: 212 N. Weigle,
Watonga, 73772
(580)623-5949

Bryan: 117 N. 3rd,
Durant, 74701
(580)924-4421

Caddo: 201 W. Oklahoma,
Anadarko, 73005
(405)247-3372

Canadian: 303 N. Choctaw,
El Reno, 73036
(405)262-0177

Carter: 20 B St.SW, Ste.202,
Ardmore, 73401
(580)223-9674

Cherokee: 213 W. Delaware,
Tahlequah, 74464
(918)456-6173

Choctaw: 300 E. Duke,
Hugo, 74743
(580)286-7611

Cimarron: Courthouse
Square, Boise City, 73933
(580)338-3604

Cleveland: 201 S. Jones,
Norman, 73069
(405)321-8268

Coal: 4 N. Main,
Coalgate, 74538
 (580)924-4421

Comanche: 316 SW 5th, Rm.
502, Lawton, 73501
(580)585-4444
Cotton: 301 N. Broadway,
Walters, 73572
(580)585-4444

Craig: 210 W. Delaware,
Vinita, 74301
(918)256-3320

Creek: 222 E. Dewey,
Rm.302, Sapulpa, 74066
(918)224-3921

Custer: 603 B. St.,
Arapaho, 73620
(580)323-3232

Delaware: 327 5th St.,
Jay, 74346
(918)253-4217

Dewey: 202 S. Broadway,
Taloga, 73667
(580)256-8616

Ellis: 100 S. Washington,
Arnett, 73832
(580)832-3144

Garfield: 114 W. Broadway,
Enid, 73701
(580)233-1311

Garvin: 201 W. Grant, Rm.
15, Pauls Valley, 73075
(405)321-8268

Grady: 217 N. 3rd St.,
Chickasha, 73018
(405)224-4770
Grant: 112 E. Guthrie, Rm.
201, Medford, 73759
(580)623-5949

Greer: 106 E. Jefferson,
Mangum, 73554
(580)782-3653

Harmon: 114 W. Hollis,
Hollis, 73550 (580)782-3653

Harper: 311 S.E. 1st,
Buffalo, 73834 (580)338-
3604
Haskell: 202 E. Main, Stigler,
74462 (918)423-1324

Hughes: 200 N. Broadway,
Holdenville, 74848
(405)379-5450

Jackson: 101 N. Main,
Altus, 73521 (580)482-5334

Jefferson: 220 N. Main, Rm.
201, Waurika, 73573
(580)228-2707

Johnston: 403 W. Main,
Ste.202, Tishomingo, 73460
(580)223-9674

Kay: 201 S. Main, Newkirk,
74647 (580)362-2571

Kingfisher: 101 S. Main,
Rm.25, Kingfisher, 73750/
(405)375-3893
Kiowa: 316 S. Main, Hobart,
73651 (580)782-3653

Latimer: 109 N. Central,
Wilburton, 74578
(918)465-3451

LeFlore: 100 S. Broadway,
Poteau, 74953
(918)647-2245

Lincoln: 811 Manvel Ave,
Ste.1, Chandler, 74834
(405)275-6800

Logan: 301 E. Harrison,
Guthrie, 73044
(405)282-0655

Love: 405 W. Main, Ste. 301,
Marietta, 73448
(580)223-9674

Major: 500 E. Broadway,
Fairview, 73737
(580)256-8616

Marshall: Courthouse Plaza,
Madill, 73446 (580)223-9674

Mayes: 1 Court Pl., Ste.250,
Pryor, 74361
(918)825-2171 McClain: 121

N.2nd, Rm.212, Purcell,
73080 (405)527-6574

McCurtain: 108 N. Central,
Idabel, 74745 (580)286-7611
McIntosh: 110 N. 1st,
Eufaula, 74432
(918)758-1218

Murray: 10th & Wyandotte,
Sulphur, 73086
(580)223-9674

Muskogee: 220 State St.,
Muskogee, 74401
(918)682-3374

Noble: 300 Courthouse Dr.
#6, Perry, 73077
(580)362-2571

Nowata: 229 N. Maple,
Nowata, 74048
(918)337-2860

Okfuskee: 3rd & Atlanta,
Okemah, 74850
(918)623-1411

Oklahoma: 320 Robert S.
Kerr, OKC, 73102
(405)713-1639

Okmulgee: 314 W. 7th,
Okmulgee, 74447
(918)758-1218

Osage: 628 1/2 S. Kihekah,
Pawhuska, 74056
(918)287-1510

Ottawa: 102 E. Central,
Ste.201, Miami, 74354
(918)542-5547
Pawnee: 500 Harrison,
Pawnee, 74058
(918)287-1511

Payne: 606 S. Husband, Rm. 111, Stillwater, 74074 (405)624-2182

Pittsburg: 109 E. Carl Albert, McAlester, 74501 (918)423-1324

Pontotoc: 105 W. 13th, Ada, 74821 (580)332-0341

Pottawatomie: 331 N. Broadway, Shawnee, 74801 (405)275-6800

Pushmataha: 302 S.W. B, Antlers, 74523 (580)286-7611

Roger Mills: 503 S. Broadway, Cheyenne, 73628 (580)832-3144

Rogers: 219 S. Missouri, Claremore, 74017 (918)341-3164

Seminole: 110 S. Wewoka, Wewoka, 74884 (405)257-3368

Sequoyah: 120 E. Chickasaw, Sallisaw, 74955 (918)775-9131

Stephens: 101 S.11th, Rm. 303, Duncan, 73533 (580)255-8726

Texas: 319 N. Main, Guymon, 73942 (580)338-3730

Tillman: 201 N. Main, Frederick, 73542 (580)482-5334

Tulsa: 500 S. Denver, Ste. 900, Tulsa, 74103 (918)596-4915
Wagoner: 307 E. Cherokee, Wagoner, 74467 (918)485-2119

Washington: 400 S. Johnstone, Bartlesville, 74003 (918)337-2860

Washita: 111 E. Main, Cordell, 73632 (580)832-3144

Woods: 407 Government St., Alva, 73717 (580)256-8616

Woodward: 1600 Main St., Ste.5, Woodward, 73801 (580)256-8616

For more information please visit: www.ok.gov/dac

Employment Rights To Survivor Of Violent Crime,

Oklahoma law states: "If the claimant separated from employment due to domestic violence or abuse, verified by any reasonable or confidential documentation, which causes the individual to reasonably believe that the individual's continued employment would jeopardize the safety of the individual or of any member of the individual's immediate family."

- If you are the Survivor of domestic violence or abuse and if it has resulted in your separation from employment, you may be eligible for Unemployment Insurance (UI) Benefits.

  - available free of charge from the Oklahoma Employment Security Commission (OESC)

  - those transitioning between careers, OESC provides training, educational opportunities, skill building, resume assistance, networking, and job referrals.

Determine your eligibility and file an UI benefit claim 1-800-555-1554 www.oesc.ok.gov. For information on reemployment www.oesc.ok.gov 1-888-980-WORK 9675).

Know Your Rights As A Survivor Of A Violent Crime:

- To be notified that a Court proceeding to which a Survivor or witness has been subpoenaed will or will not go on as scheduled, in order to save the person an unnecessary trip to Court;

- To receive protection from harm and threats of harm arising out of the cooperation of the person with law enforcement and prosecution efforts, and to be provided with information as to the level of protection available and how to access protection;

- To be informed of financial assistance and other social services available as a result of being a witness or a crime Survivor, including information on how to apply for the assistance and services;

- To be informed of procedure to be followed in order to apply for and receive any witness fee to which the Survivor or witness is entitled;

- To be informed of the procedure to be followed in order to apply for and receive any restitution to which the Survivor is entitled;

- To be provided, whenever possible, a secure waiting area during Court proceedings that does not require close proximity to defendants and families and friends of defendants;

- To have any stolen or other personal property expeditiously returned by law enforcement agencies when no longer needed as evidence. If feasible, all such property, except weapons, currency, contraband, property subject to evidentiary analysis and property the ownership of which is disputed, shall be returned to the person;

- To be provided with appropriate employer intercession services to ensure that employers of the Survivors and witnesses will cooperate with the criminal justice process in order to minimize the loss of pay and other Benefits of the employee resulting from Court appearances;

- To have all family members of all homicide Survivors afforded the services under this section, whether or not the person is to be a witness to any criminal proceedings;

- To be informed of any plea bargaining negotiations;

- To have Survivor impact statements filed with the judgment and sentence;

- To be informed if a sentence is overturned, remanded for a new trial or otherwise modified by the Oklahoma Court of Criminal Appeals;

- To be informed in writing of all statutory rights;

- To be informed when any family member is required to be a witness by subpoena from the defense, there must be a showing that the witness can provide relevant testimony as to the guilt or innocence of the defendant before the witness may be excluded from the proceeding by invoking the rule to remove potential witnesses;

- To be notified by the Pardon and Parole Board of Pardon and Parole actions if you request notification;

- To be informed of felony cases involving violent crime or sex offenses when pre-trial proceedings may substantially delay prosecution;

- To protect the identity of the Survivor in sexual assault cases;

- To request that the offender be tested for sexually transmitted diseases in sexual assault cases as ordered by the Court;

- To be informed that any sentence, including Life Without Parole, may be commuted;

- To receive written notification of how to access Survivor rights information from the interviewing officer or investigating detective; and

- To speedy disposition of the charges free from unwarranted delay caused by or at the behest of the defendant or minor.

For more information on your rights and other useful resources please visit www.ok.gov/dac and click on the Just for Survivors tab.

What Type Of Financial Assistance May Be Available For Survivors Of Violent Crime?

Out of pocket expenses considered under the Crime Survivors Compensation Program are:

- Medical and dental care
- Prescriptions
- Counseling and rehabilitation
- Work loss or loss of support
- Caregiver work loss
- Crime scene clean-up
- Funeral and burial expense
- Property loss and pain and suffering are not covered
- No attorney is needed to file a claim
- No arrest or conviction is required
- You must cooperate fully with law enforcement
- Para revisar esta información en Español, por favour visite la pagina web www.ok.gov/dac. Oprima donde dice Survivor Services y luego oprima Español (la sexta opción)

Education Outreach
Outreach Center

TCC's Education Outreach Center
A place for anyone to learn more about TCC and receive personalized attention throughout the application process. Beginning August 5th our fall office hours are:
Monday - Thursday 8:00 AM - 5:00 PM
Friday 10:00 AM - 5:00 PM
Saturday 9:00 AM - 3:00 PM
918-595-2020
outreach.center@tulsacc.edu

El Centro de Education y Alcance a la Comunidad es UN lugar para cualquier persona que esté interesada en aprender más acerca de cómo empezar el proceso de aplicación para la universidad. Nuestras horas de oficina Son:
Lunes - Jueves 8:00 AM - 5:00 PM
Viernes 10:00 AM - 5:00 PM
Sabado 9:00 AM - 3:00 PM
918-595-2020
outreach.center@tulsacc.edu

Services Offered?
- General information about TCC
- Assistance completing the application process
- Help filling out the FASFA and other scholarship applications
- College Placement Testing
- Career counseling/advisement
- Assistance setting up class schedules & enrollment
- Computer lab with Internet access & Printer
- On-Site College Classes
- On-Site English as a Second Language Classes

¿Que Servicios Ofrecemos?
- Arena más acerca de TCC y cómo empezar la universidad
- Asistencia para completar el proceso de admisión
- Asistencia para completar las aplicaciones para ayuda financiera
- Examen de ubicación para universidad y también para las Clases de Ingles
- Tenemos consejeros para ayudarle a escoger una carrera
- Le ayudamos a acomodar su horario de clases y procesar la Inscripción
- Tenemos computadoras con acceso a internet
- Ofrecemos clases de universidad

Union Public Schools:

This Program Offers Classes in GED Preparation, English As A Second Language (ESL), and Family and Workplace Literacy. The Program Also Administers the Official GED Exam.

All of the Union Adult Education Instructors Have Attained Their Certification and Many Are State Trainers in Their Field.

Contact
Located at the northwest corner of the Union 9th Grade Center(formerly Intermediate High)
7616 South Garnett Road
Broken Arrow, OK 74012
918.357.7040
Monday - Thursday 8:00am - 5:00pm during the summer

Services Offered

- **GED Preparation**
  - **Classes are provided for adults who are no longer attending high school and need basic skills instruction in reading, writing, math, and life skills.**
- **GED and Industry Certification Exams**
  - **Passing the General Educational Development or GED test qualifies adults to receive a high school diploma issued by the State of Oklahoma and participate in our graduation ceremony. This exam is available on paper or computer. We also offer certification exams for various fields such as IT, health, and education through our Pearson VUE testing center.**
- **English as a Second Language**
  - **English as a Second Language(ESL) classes provide instruction to non-English-speaking adults. Students learn communication and**

assimilation skills in order to be productive citizens.
- Family Literacy
  - Family Literacy classes offer ABE and ESL to parents along with parent/child interaction time. By learning together as a family, the program reinforces life skills that parents and children need to succeed.

- Workplace Literacy
  - These classes are designed specifically to teach ABE or ESL to employees in order to achieve high performance work and product quality. Union's instruction staff will identify tasks important to the employer and make those tasks the focus of basic skills.

Employment Workforce Development
Youth Workforce Development

Kim Braddy
www.workforceok.org/locator.htm
Email: kim.braddy@oesc.state.ok.us

Not only can youth learn about the world of work (and often find their first job) through local youth programs; but can also participate in academic enrichment, leadership development, and college & career exploration. Special programs are available for school dropouts, homeless youth, runaways, youth in or aging out of foster care, pregnant and/or parenting youth, offenders, youth with disabilities, youth who may be basic skills deficient, and youth in need of additional assistance to complete an educational program or to secure and hold employment.

The Following Ten Services are Offered to Oklahoma's Youth, Ages 14 to 21:
- Tutoring, study skills training, and instruction leading to secondary school completion, including dropout prevention strategies;
- Alternative secondary school offerings;
  - Summer employment opportunities directly linked to academic and occupational learning;
  - Paid and unpaid work experience including internships and job shadowing;
  - Occupational skills training;

- Leadership development opportunities, which may include such activities as positive social behavior and soft skills, decision-making, teamwork and other activities;
- Supportive services which may include assistance with work tools, uniforms, child care, or transportation;
- Adult mentoring for the period of participation and a subsequent period, for a total of not less than 12 months;
- Follow up services; and,
- Comprehensive guidance and counseling which may include drug and alcohol abuse counseling and referral, as appropriate.

WIA Youth Service Providers
Workforce Oklahoma - Reno Center
416 Hudiburg Circle, Suite B
Oklahoma City, OK 73108
Telephone Number: 405-639-3640
Fax Number: 405-639-3682
Contact: Ollivet Brothers
ollivettbrothers@arboret.com

*Additional Office Locations:
7401 NE 23rd St., OKC
1141 E. Main St., Norman
219 S. Broad St., Guthrie

Counties served: Logan, Oklahoma, Cleveland
Youth and Family Services
7565 East Hwy 66
PO Box 1207
El Reno OK 73036
Contact: irk Huff
kirk.huff@yfsok.org

(405) 262-6555 - FAX (405) 262-6557

Counties served: Canadian
Workforce Dynamics, Inc.
14101 Acme Rd
Shawnee OK 74804
Contact: Debi Reid
debireid@sbcglobal.net
(405) 878-0759 - FAX (405) 878-1369

Counties served: Cherokee, Adair, Sequoyah, Muskogee,
McIntosh and Wagoner, Okmulgee
Payne County Youth Services, Inc.
2224 W 12th St
Stillwater OK 74074
Contact: Roberta Douglas
robertad@pcys.org
(405) 377-3380 - FAX (405) 377-3499

Counties served: Payne
Northern Oklahoma Youth Services
2203 N Ash
Ponca City OK 74601
Contact: April Goodwin
noys_april@sbcglobal.net
(580) 762-8341 FAX (580) 762-9967

Counties served: Kay
Youth and Family Services
7565 East Hwy 66
PO Box 1207
El Reno OK 73036
Contact: Kirk Huff

kirk.huff@yfsok.org
(405) 262-6555 - FAX (405) 262-6557

Counties served: Kingfisher, Blaine, Alfalfa, Garfield, Grant, Major
Dynamic Educational Systems Inc. (DESI)
104 Hester Place
Chelsea OK 74016
Contact: Michelle Bish
michelle.bish@oesc.state.ok.us
(918) 789-2574 - FAX (918) 789-2400

Counties Served: Washington, Nowata, Craig, Ottawa, Rogers, Mayes, Delaware
Oklahoma Economic Development Authority (OEDA)
PO Box 668 330 Douglas Ave
Beaver OK 73932
Contact: Mike Bostic: oedaxdir@ptsi.net
(580) 625-4531

Counties served: Cimarron, Texas, Beaver, Harper, Woods, Woodward, Dewey, Ellis
Arbor Education & Training, LLC
14002 E. 21st St, Suite 1030
Tulsa OK 74120
Contact: Brad Williams
bradleywilliams@arboret.com
(918) 796-1232 - FAX (918) 796-1233

Counties Served: Caddo, Grady, McClain, Comanche, Stephens, Jefferson, Cotton, Tillman
Kiamichi Economic Development District of Oklahoma (KEDDO)
PO Box 328
Wilburton OK 74578

Contact: Danny Baldwin
dbaldwin@keddo.org
(918) 465-2367 FAX (918) 465-3873

Counties Served: Pittsburg, Haskell, Latimer, Leflore,
Pushmataha, McCurtain, Choctaw
Big Five Community Services, Inc.
PO Box 1577 Durant OK 74702
Contact: Lorrie Wright lwright@bigfive.org
(580) 924-5331 - FAX (580) 924-2004

Counties Served: Garvin, Pontotoc, Coal, Atoka, Johnston,
Murray, Carter, Love, Marshall, Bryan
South Western Oklahoma Development Authority (SWODA)
PO Box 569 420 Sooner Drive Burns Flat OK 7
Contact: Jana Harris,
Director of Community & Economic Development
jana@swoda.org
(580) 562-4882 FAX (580) 562-4880
Counties Served: Tulsa, Creek, Pawnee, and Osage
Arbor Education & Training, LLC
14002 E 21St, Suite 1030
Tulsa OK 74120
Contact: Brad Williams
bradleywilliams@arboret.com
(918) 796-1232 - FAX (918) 796-1233

Incentives for Employers
Work Opportunity Tax Credit
What You Need to Know to Save Up to $2,400 per Employee on
Federal Taxes

What is the Work Opportunity Tax Credit?
The Work Opportunity Tax Credit is a tax credit offered to

employers as an incentive to hire individuals who are members of targeted groups which have traditionally faced significant barriers to employment.

1. **The Small Business and Title IV-A Recipient** - a member of a family that has received assistance from Aid to Dependent Children (AFDC) or its successor program Temporary Assistance to Needy Families (TANF) for any 9 months within the last 18 months.
2. **Veteran/Disabled Veteran/Unemployed Veteran** - a veteran and member of a family that received food stamps for at least three of the 15 months preceding the date of hire, **or** a disabled veteran who is entitled to a service-connected disability and has a hiring date which is not more than one year after having been discharged **or** released from active duty in the Armed Forces of the United States **or** has aggregate periods of unemployment during the one year period ending on the hiring date that equals or exceeds six months.
3. **Ex-Felon** - a person convicted of a felony AND within the past year was either convicted or released from prison. (The requirement to meet the Lower Living Income standard has been removed)
4. **Designated Community Resident** – is an individual who attained age 18 but not yet 40 on the hiring date and his/her principal place of abode (residing) within an Enterprise Zone, Empowerment Community or a Rural Renewal County.
5. **Vocational Rehabilitation Recipient** - a person with a disability who has received or is receiving vocational rehabilitation from a rehabilitation agency approved by the State or the Department of Veterans Affairs. (Drug/alcohol rehab does not qualify.) Also including a Ticket to Work holder who has an Individual Work Plan with an employment network agency.
6. **Summer Youth/Disconnected Youth** - a person a least age 16 but not 18 on the hiring date and who has a principal

residence in an Empowerment Community or Enterprise Zone. (During 90-day summer working period.)

7. **Food Stamp Recipient** - a person who is at least 18 but under age 40, AND is a member of a family that has received food stamps for the last 6 months; OR received food stamps for at least three of the last 5 months, AND is no longer eligible to receive them.

8. **SSI Recipient** - a person receiving Supplemental Security Income (SSI) Benefits for any month during the 60 days preceding the date of hire.

9. **Long-term Family Assistance Recipients** – a qualified long-term family assistance recipients is an individual certified by a designated local agency as being: (1) a member of a family that has received family assistance for at least 18 consecutive months ending on the hiring date; (2) a member of a family that has received such family assistance for a total of at least 18 months (whether or not consecutive) after August 5, 1997 (the date of enactment of the welfare-to-work tax credit) if the individual is hired within two years after the date that the 18 month total is reached; or (3) a member of a family who is no longer eligible for family assistance because of either Federal or State time limits, if the individual is hired with two years after the Federal or State time limits made the family ineligible for family assistance.

Special Excepted Appointment (SEA) Project-Hire People with Disabilities

People with disabilities may obtain employment with the Federal government through a number of avenues including the SEA project which was developed to provide an alternate route to employment for people with severe disabilities.

To qualify for an excepted appointment you must meet certain criteria:

Have the basic knowledge, skills and abilities for the job and be able to perform the duties of the job with or without reasonable accommodation.

1. Have an impairment which substantially limits one or more major life activities; have a record of such an impairment; or regarded as having such an impairment.

2. Have a State vocational rehabilitation counselor or visual services counselor certify that you have the ability to do the job and do it without risk to yourself or others. The certification must be supported by medical documentation regarding the severity of your disability.

WORKFORCE OKLAHOMA Centers and Federal agencies in the Oklahoma City Metropolitan area are working together to create a pool of Federal job applicants. When an individual with a disability makes application at one of the Workforce Oklahoma offices, their Federal job application can be considered by all agencies participating in the SEA project.

Ask your Workforce Representative at any WORKFORCE OKLAHOMA Center for a SEA application packet.

Federal Bonding- "At-risk", Hard-to-place Job Seekers

David Slump
david.slimp@oesc.state.ok.us
(405) 557-5374

This program provides Fidelity Bonds that guarantee honesty for "at-risk", hard-to-place job seekers. The bonds issued by the FBP serve as a job placement tool by guaranteeing to the employer the job honesty of at-risk job seekers.

Employers receive the bonds free-or-charge as incentive to hire hard-to-place job applicants as wage earners. The FBP bond insurance was designed to reimburse the employer for any loss due to employee theft of money or property with no deductible amount to become the employer's liability (i.e., 100% bond insurance coverage).

Adult and Dislocated Worker
Jackie Younger, (405) 557-5314

WIA funds are appropriated through the Employment and Training Division to provide core, intensive and training services through Oklahoma's Workforce Investment System.

- Laid off from a long-term job and has very little hope of returning to that employer or industry. He or she could have been an unpaid caregiver to the family and dependent upon someone else's income

- Self-employed workers who have faced natural disasters or local economic downturns also qualify for help under this program

- 18 years or older

- Has been terminated or laid off (or has received notice of a termination or lay off)

- Eligible for unemployment or have exhausted unemployment Benefits

- May have worked for and extended time in a job that did not provide unemployment insurance Benefits

- May be unlikely to return to a previous industry or occupation

- Could have lost a job or received a notice of layoff due to a closure or substantial layoff – or received a notice of general layoff within 180 days

- May have been self-employed, like a farmer, rancher, or fisherman, yet because of local economic conditions or a natural disaster, that source of employment has ended

- A displaced homemaker

Full-service, comprehensive centers have Career Resource Centers, an area set aside for self-help, or limited assistance, much like a community library. That provide computers and software for you to prepare a resume, for instance, with books and videos nearby to guide you. If you find that you need additional help, a staff member is always available to you.

Core Services May Include:

- Employment information, including job vacancy listings, skills necessary to obtain employment in specific jobs, and earnings and skill requirements for occupations in the local, regional and national labor markets.

- Information regarding filing claims for unemployment compensation.

- Eligibility determination for services requiring criteria-tested eligibility.

- Outreach and orientation to Workforce Center services.

- Information on eligible training providers & Information on supportive services.

Work-Based Training, Age 55 and Older
Senior Community Service Employment Program (SCSEP)

The SCSEP provides training and employment services to eligible low-income jobseekers age 55 and older who have poor employment prospects. Program participants gain competitive job skills through paid part-time work-based training at non-profit organizations such as day-care centers, senior centers, schools and hospitals, and governmental entities such as city, county, State, and Federal agencies. Participants "earn while they learn" new skills and provide valuable community services. SCSEP also assists program participants to find and secure unsubsidized employment with public and private entities.

Program participants work an average of 20 hours per week, and are paid Federal minimum wage. These community service experiences are intended to serve as a bridge to unsubsidized employment positions.

Eligible Participants: Program participants must be at least 55 and have a famiily income of no more than 125% over the Federal poverty level. Enrollment priority is given to persons over age 60, Veterans, and qualified spouses of Veterans. Preference is given to eligible minority, limited English-speaking, and Native American individuals. Preference is also given to eligible individuals who have the greatest economic need.

Employment and Career Website:
Online Career Assessments:
http://www.onetonline.org/

http://www.mynextmove.org/

http://www.mynextmove.org/vets/

Registered Apprentiship Programs:
The Registered Apprenticeship system provides the opportunity for workers seeking high-skilled, high- paying jobs and for employers seeking to build a qualified workforce. In this regard, the Registered Apprenticeship system effectively meets the needs of both employ

Registered Apprenticeship is highly active in traditional industries such as construction and manufacturing, but it is also instrumental in the training and development of emerging industries such as healthcare, energy, and homeland security.

It's an Immediate Job

Apprentices start working from day one with incremental wage increases as they become more proficient on-the-job. Apprenticeships range from one to six years, but the majority are

four years in length. In 2011, more than 130,000 individuals nationwide became apprentices.

It's On-the-Job Learning and Education

The "Earn and Learn" training model of Registered Apprenticeship provides a unique combination of structured learning with on-the-job training from an assigned mentor. Related instruction, technical training or other certified training is provided by apprenticeship training centers, technical schools, community colleges, and/or institutions employing distance and computer-based learning approaches. The goal is to provide workers with advanced skillsets that meet the specific needs of employers."

It's a Credential

Upon completion of a Registered Apprenticeship program, participants receive an industry issued, nationally recognized credential that certifies occupational proficiency, is portable, and can provide a pathway to the middle class. In many cases, these programs provide apprentices with the opportunity to simultaneously obtain secondary and post-secondary degrees. In 2011, over 55,000 participants nationwide graduated from a Registered Apprenticeship program.

For More Information Log On:

http://www.doleta.gov/OA/apprenticeship.cfm

Locate Apprentiship Programs in Your State:
https://pathwaystosuccess.workforce3one.org/map.aspx

The Registered Apprenticeship system has been utilized to meet the needs of America's skilled workforce for over 75 years. It is a unique, flexible training system that combines job related technical instruction with structured on-the-job learning experiences.

Registered Apprenticeship is a leader in preparing American workers to compete in a global 21st Century economy because the system keeps pace with advancing technologies and innovations in training and human resource development.

Veterans in Apprenticeship

Helmets to Hardhats is a national, non-profit program that connects National Guard, Reserve, retired and transitioning active duty military service members with skilled training and quality career opportunities in the construction industry. Most career opportunities offered by the program are connected to federally-approved apprenticeship training programs. www.helmetstohardhats.org

Veterans in Piping is an apprenticeship program that offers high-quality skills training and jobs in the pipe trades to US Veterans and active duty military personnel preparing to leave the service. Participants enroll in accelerated 18-week courses in welding and/or HVACR service. Participants also earn industry-recognized certifications as a part of their education. www.uavip.org

The Painters and Allied Trades Veterans Program assists transitioning Veterans from military service to civilian careers in the finishing trades industry. The International Union of Painters and Allied Trades is dedicated to providing service men and women the tools necessary to be successful in a rewarding career in construction.www.pat-vp.org

Farmworker's Employment Rights

If you believe that your agricultural employment rights have been violated, below are links to information on filing a Complaint or Toll-Free Numbers to call if you have questions.

If farmworkers have a Complaint about an American Job Center (also commonly referred to as a One-Stop Career Center) or a job they were referred t

Contact the local American Job Center manager (locate centers at http://www.servicelocator.org/), or Contact Mr. Juan M. Regalado,

National Monitor Advocate

U.S. Department of Labor, Employment and Training Administration
90 7th Street Room 17-300,
San Francisco, Ca. 94103
Telephone: (415) 625-7904
Fax: (415) 625-7923 Email: nma@dol.gov

Department of Labor, Wage and Hour Division
1-866-487-9243

Department of Labor, Occupational Safety & Health Administration
1-800-321-6742

Department of Labor, Office of Foreign Labor Certification –
302-886-8000

Environmental Protection Agency –
1-800-222-1222

Department of Justice, Civil Rights Div. Office of Special Counsel
–
1-800-255-7688

Department of Agriculture –1-866-632-9992

Housing Opportunities for Farmworkers National Housing Directory

U.S. Department of Labor
Employment and Training Administration
Office of Workforce Investment
Division of National Programs, Tools and Technical Assistance
Specialty

National Programs Unit
200 Constitution Avenue, NW Room C-4510
Washington, DC 20210
Phone Number: 202-693-3045

Community Resources and
Housing Development
Corporation Arizona,
Colorado, Idaho, New
Mexico
Mr. Al Gold
Executive Director
303-428-1448

Florida Non-Profit Housing,
Inc. Delaware, Florida,
Maryland, Mississippi,
Virginia
Mr. Selvin McGahee
Executive Director 863-385-
2519

Farmworker Coordinating
Council of Palm Beach, Inc.
Florida (Belle Glade,
Pahokee, Canal Point &
South Bay)
Mr. Sergio Palacio
Executive Director 561-533-
7227

Motivation Education and
Training Inc. Louisiana,
Texas Mr. F. Luis Esparza Jr.
Executive Director 281-689-
5544

ORO Development
Corporation Oklahoma
Mr. Jorge Martinez Executive
Director
405-840-7077

Office of Rural and
Farmworker Housing
Oregon, Washington Mr.
Marty Miller Executive
Director
509-248-7014

People's Self-Help Housing
Corporation California
(Central Coast)
Mr. John Fowler CFO
805-540-2462

PPEP
Microbusiness and Housing
Development Corporation
Arizona (Yuma County)
Ms. Kari Hogan
Chief Administrative Officer
520-770-2500

Proteus Incorporation Iowa
Ms. Jesus Soto
Chief Executive Officer
515-271-5303

Pathstone Corporation
Indiana,

Maine, New Jersey, New
York,
 Ohio, Pennsylvania,
Puerto Rico,Vermont
Ms. John Wiltse
Senior Operations Director
585-340-3346
Rural Community Assistance
Corporation Hawaii (Oahu)
Mr. Finnly Sutton
Senior Operations Director
775-246-5404
South City Housing
Corporation California
(Monterey County, Soledad
City)
Ms. Sandi Hollenbeck
Management Analyst
408-843-9239

SELF-Help Enterprises
California (San Joaquin
Valley)
Mr. Thomas Collishaw
Vice President and Director
of Development 559-802-
1620

Telamon Corporation (NC)
Alabama, Delaware,
Georgia,

Maryland, North Carolina,
South Carolina,Virginia,
West Virginia
Mr. Donna Ryder
Housing Director
919-239-8157

Telamon Corporation (MI)
Michigan Mr. Donald
Kuchnicki
State Director 517-323-7002

Tennessee Opportunity
Program
Tennessee Ms. Gaila
Fletcher
 Executive Director
615-459-3600

United Migrant Opportunity
Services (UMOS)
Illinois, Iowa, Kansas,
Minnesota,
Missouri, Nebraska, South
Dakota, Wisconsin
Mr. Leonardo Martinez
Vice Preisdent of Operations
608-334-2221

Employment and Training Administration
U.S. Department of Labor | Frances Perkins Building, 200
Constitution Ave., NW, Washington, DC 20210

www.doleta.gov | Telephone: 1-877-US-2JOBS (1-877-872-5627)
| TTY |
Fax: 1-202-693-2726 | C

Fair Housing
What Professionals Need To Know About Fair Housing

Federal fair housing law consists of the Civil Rights Act of 1866 and Title VIII of the Civil Rights Act of 1968, otherwise known as the Fair Housing Act. The act, as amended in 1988, provides that no one can be discriminated against in the sale, rental, or financing of residential dwellings on the basis of these protected classes:

> *TIP: Fair housing laws in some states and municipalities may include additional protected classes—such as sexual preference, age, or sources of income. For information on your State's fair housing laws, contact your State housing authority or visit the U.S. Department of Housing and Urban Development online. The site has a section for real estate brokers and a listing of State HUD offices.*

- Race
- Color
- Religion
- Sex
- Handicap
- Familial status
- National origin
- In addition, the Civil Rights Act of 1866 provides that all U.S. citizens have the same rights as white citizens to "inherit, purchase, sell, hold, and convey real and personal property."

The U.S. Supreme Court has interpreted this act to prohibit **all forms of racial discrimination** with regard to real estate—even discrimination by private individuals. Penalties can include punitive as well as actual damages.

TIP: The handicapped category under the Fair Housing Act includes not only obvious physical handicaps, but mental handicaps, alcoholism, and AIDS. Current abusers of controlled substances are not covered.

Exceptions to the Rules
1. An owner who sells or rents a single-family home without the services of a real estate practitioner is exempt from coverage if he or she does not own or have an interest in more than three single-family houses and does not advertise.

2. Owners of buildings designed for occupancy by up to four families are exempt from the Fair Housing Act as long as they live in one of the rental units and do not use any advertising or hire real estate professionals. However, discrimination on the basis of race is never lawful.

3. Owners or managers of qualified "housing for older persons" may refuse to rent to families with children. To qualify, a property must have at least 80 percent of the units occupied by at least one person 55 years of age or older and be marketed to those 55 or older.

TIP: Get a statement that a property meets these requirements from the current owner before you begin marketing it to seniors.

4. Religious organizations may discriminate in the sale, rental, or occupancy of their noncommercial property.

5. Private clubs may limit the rental or occupancy of their noncommercial lodgings to members.

Fair Housing Compliance Checklist

Use this checklist to make sure you're complying with the Fair Housing Act.

If you answer "no" to any of the questions below, consider adjusting your practices accordingly.

- ☐ Do you have a written fair housing policy?
- ☐ Do you publicize your commitment to fair housing in your office and in your advertising to clients?
- ☐ Is fair housing training required in your company?
- ☐ Have you developed procedures to provide equal professional service?
- ☐ Do you review your offices' compliance with your procedures regularly?
- ☐ Do you have a corrective action policy?
- ☐ Do you regularly review and modify your procedures to respond to changes in fair housing laws and to correct deficiencies in your office?
- ☐ Do you have a way to gather feedback from customers and prospects?

Create a Fair Housing Policy Statement

Keep It Legal: The U.S. Department of Housing and Urban Development regulations require that you display a fair housing poster at your place of business where homes are sold or rented.

Have a written fair housing statement and hand a copy of it to every prospective client. It should say unequivocally that you support all applicable laws, and State specifically what the provisions of those laws are.

For example:
"This company conducts business in accordance with all Federal, State, and local fair housing laws. It is our policy to provide housing opportunities to all persons regardless of race, color, religion, sex, familial status, handicap, national origin or sexual orientation. The company's fair housing procedures are not recommendations. They must be followed by everyone associated with the company."

What Consumers Need To Know About The Fair Housing Act

When you apply for housing, you cannot be discriminated against based on your:

- o Race
- o Color
- o Religion
- o National origin
- o Sex
- o Familial status, or
- o Disability.

Where Your Rights Violated?

Has anyone taken any of the following actions based on race, color, religion, national origin, sex, familial status, or disability:·

- ☐ Refuse to rent or sell housing
- ☐ Refuse to negotiate for housing
- ☐ Set different terms, conditions, or privileges for sale/rental of a dwelling
- ☐ Falsely deny that housing is available for inspection, sale, or rental
- ☐ Deny anyone access to or membership in a facility or service related to the sale or rental of housing

- ☐ Refuse to make a mortgage loan or discriminate in appraising property
- ☐ Refuse to provide information regarding loans
- ☐ Impose different terms or conditions on a loan
- ☐ Threaten, coerce, intimidate, or interfere with anyone exercising a fair housing right or assisting others who exercise that right
- ☐ Advertise or make any statement that indicates a limitation or preference based on those characteristics. (This particular prohibition applies to single-family and owner-occupied housing that is otherwise not controlled by the Fair Housing Act)

If you answer "yes" to any of the questions above, consider filing a Complaint at the numbers below.

Additional Protection if You Have a Disability

If you or someone associated with you:

Have a physical or mental disability (including hearing, mobility and visual impairments, chronic alcoholism, chronic mental illness, AIDS, AIDS Related Complex and mental retardation) that substantially limits one or more major life activities

Have a record of such a disability or are regarded as having such a disability
your landlord may not:

- ☐ Refuse to let you make reasonable modifications to your dwelling or common use areas, at your expense, if necessary for the disabled person to use the housing. (Where reasonable, the landlord may permit changes only if you agree to restore the property to its original condition when you move.)

- Refuse to make reasonable accommodations in rules, policies, practices or services if necessary for the disabled person to use the housing.

Example: A building with a no pets policy must allow a visually impaired tenant to keep a guide dog.

Example: An apartment complex that offers tenants ample, unassigned parking must honor a request from a mobility-impaired tenant for a reserved space near her apartment if necessary to assure that she can have access to her apartment.

However, housing need not be made available to a person who is a direct threat to the health or safety of others or who currently uses illegal drugs.

In The Sale And Rental Of Housing:

No one may take any of the following actions based on race, color, national origin, religion, sex, familial status or handicap:

- Refuse to rent or sell housing
- Refuse to negotiate for housing
- Make housing unavailable
- Deny a dwelling
- Set different terms, conditions or privileges for sale or rental of a dwelling
- Provide different housing services or facilities
- Falsely deny that housing is available for inspection, sale, or rental
- For profit, persuade owners to sell or rent (blockbusting)
- Deny anyone access to or membership in a facility or service (such as a multiple listing service) related to the sale or rental of housing

- In Mortgage Lending: No one may take any of the following actions based on race, color, national origin, religion, sex, familial status or handicap (disability):

Refuse to Make a Mortgage Loan
- Refuse to provide information regarding loans
- Impose different terms or conditions on a loan, such as different interest rates, points, or fees
- Discriminate in appraising property
- Refuse to purchase a loan
- Set different terms or conditions for purchasing a loan
- In Addition: It is illegal for anyone to:
- Threaten, coerce, intimidate or interfere with anyone exercising a fair housing right or assisting others who exercise that right
- Advertise or make any statement that indicates a limitation or preference based on race, color, national origin, religion, sex, familial status, or handicap. This prohibition against discriminatory advertising applies to single-family and owner-occupied housing that is otherwise exempt from the Fair Housing Act
- Requirements for New Buildings

In Buildings That are Ready for First Occupancy After March 13, 1991, and Have an Elevator and Four or More Units:

- Public and common areas must be accessible to persons with disabilities.
- Doors and hallways must be wide enough for wheelchairs.
- All units must have:
- An accessible route into and through the unit.
- Accessible light switches, electrical outlets, thermostats and other environmental controls.

☐ Reinforced bathroom walls to allow later installation of grab bars.

☐ Kitchens and bathrooms that can be used by people in wheelchairs.

☐ If a building with four or more units has no elevator and will be ready for first occupancy after March 13, 1991, these standards apply to ground floor units.

☐ These requirements for new buildings do not replace any more stringent standards in State or local law.

Housing Opportunities for Families

Unless a building or community qualifies as housing for older persons, it may not discriminate based on familial status. That is, it may not discriminate against families in which one or more children under 18 live with:

☐ A parent.

☐ A person who has legal custody of the child or children or.

☐ The designee of the parent or legal custodian, with the parent or custodian's written permission.

☐ Familial status protection also applies to pregnant women and anyone securing legal custody of a child under 18.

Exemption: Housing for older persons is exempt from the prohibition against familial status discrimination if:

The HUD Secretary has determined that it is specifically designed for and occupied by:

☐ *Elderly persons under a Federal, State or local government program.*

☐ *It is occupied solely by persons who are 62 or older or.*

☐ *It houses at least one person who is 55 or older in at least 80 percent of the occupied units, and adheres to a policy that demonstrates an intent to house persons who are 55 or older.*

☐ *A transition period permits residents on or before September 13, 1988, to continue living in the housing, regardless of their age, without interfering with the exemption.*

If You Think Your Rights Have Been Violated

HUD is ready to help with any problem of housing discrimination. If you think your rights have been violated, the Housing Discrimination Complaint Form is available for you to download, complete and return, or complete online and submit, or you may write HUD a letter, or telephone the HUD Office nearest you.

You have one year after an alleged violation to file a Complaint with HUD, but you should file it as soon as possible.

What to Tell HUD:

Your name and address
The name and address of the person your Complaint is against (the respondent)
The address or other identification to the housing involved
A short description to the alleged violation (the event that caused you to believe your rights were violated)
The date(s) to the alleged violation
Where to Write or Call:

Send the Housing Discrimination Complaint Form or a letter to the HUD Office nearest you or you may call that office directly.

If You're Disabled:

HUD also provides:

A toll-free TTY phone for the hearing impaired: 1-800-927-9275.

✓ Interpreters
✓ Tapes and braille materials
✓ Assistance in reading and completing forms

What Happens when you file a Complaint?

1. HUD will notify you when it receives your Complaint

2. Notify the alleged violator of your Complaint and permit that person to submit an answer

3. Investigate your Complaint and determine whether there is reasonable cause to believe the Fair Housing Act has been violated

4. Notify you if it cannot complete an investigation within 100 days of receiving your Complaint

5. Conciliation- HUD will try to reach an agreement with the person your Complaint is against (the respondent)

   a. A conciliation agreement must protect both you and the public interest. If an agreement is signed, HUD will take no further action on your Complaint.
   b. However, if HUD has reasonable cause to believe that a conciliation agreement is breached, HUD will recommend that the Attorney General file suit.

Complaint Referrals

If HUD has determined that your State or local agency has the same fair housing powers as HUD, HUD will refer your Complaint to that agency for investigation and notify you of the referral. That agency must begin work on your Complaint within 30 days or HUD may take it back.

What if You Need Help Quickly?

1. If you need immediate help to stop a serious problem that is being caused by a Fair Housing Act violation, HUD may be able to assist you as soon as you file a Complaint. HUD may authorize the Attorney General to go to Court to seek temporary or preliminary relief, pending the outcome of your Complaint, if:

2. Irreparable harm is likely to occur without HUD's intervention
There is substantial evidence that a violation of the Fair Housing Act occurred

   Example: A builder agrees to sell a house but, after learning the buyer is black, fails to keep the agreement. The buyer files a Complaint with HUD. HUD may authorize the Attorney General to go to Court to prevent a sale to any other buyer until HUD investigates the Complaint.

What Happens after a Complaint Investigation?

If, after investigating your Complaint, HUD finds reasonable cause to believe that discrimination occurred, it will inform you. Your case will be heard in an administrative hearing within 120 days, unless you or the respondent want the case to be heard in Federal District Court. Either way, there is no cost to you.

The Administrative Hearing:

- If your case goes to an administrative hearing HUD attorneys will litigate the case on your behalf. You may intervene in the case and be represented by your own attorney if you wish. An Administrative Law Judge (ALA) will consider evidence from you and the respondent. If the

ALA decides that discrimination occurred, the respondent can be ordered:

- To compensate you for actual damages, including humiliation, pain and suffering.

- To provide injunctive or other equitable relief, for example, to make the housing available to you.

- To pay the Federal Government a civil penalty to vindicate the public interest. The maximum penalties are $16,000 for a first violation and $65,000 for a third violation within seven years.

- To pay reasonable attorney's fees and costs.

Federal District Court

- If you or the respondent choose to have your case decided in Federal District Court, the Attorney General will file a suit and litigate it on your behalf. Like the ALA, the District Court can order relief, and award actual damages, attorney's fees and costs. In addition, the Court can award punitive damages.

- In Addition: You May File Suit: You may file suit, at your expense, in Federal District Court or State Court within two years of an alleged violation. If you cannot afford an attorney, the Court may appoint one for you. You may bring suit even after filing a Complaint, if you have not signed a conciliation agreement and an Administrative Law Judge has not started a hearing. A Court may award actual and punitive damages and attorney's fees and costs.

Other Tools to Combat Housing Discrimination:

- If there is noncompliance with the order of an Administrative Law Judge, HUD may seek temporary relief, enforcement of the order or a restraining order in a United States Court of Appeals.

- The Attorney General may file a suit in a Federal District Court if there is reasonable cause to believe a pattern or practice of housing discrimination is occurring.

For Further Information:
The Fair Housing Act and HUD's regulations contain more detail and technical information. If you need a copy of the law or regulations, contact the HUD Office nearest you.

Contact Information

Unsure? Questions? Let us know, we're here to help!

If You Live In The Following Areas/States:	Call The Toll-free Telephone Number	HUD Regional Office*
Connecticut, Maine, Massachusetts, New Hampshire, Rhode Island, Vermont	(800) 827-5005	Boston
New Jersey, New York, Puerto Rico, Virgin Islands	(800) 496-4294	New York
Delaware, District of Columbia, Maryland, Pennsylvania, Virginia, West Virginia	(888)799-2085	Philadelphia
Alabama, Florida, Georgia, Kentucky, Mississippi, North Carolina, South Carolina, Tennessee	(800) 440-8091	Atlanta
Illinois, Indiana, Michigan, Minnesota, Ohio, Wisconsin	(800) 765-9372	Chicago
Arkansas, Louisiana, New Mexico, Oklahoma, Texas	(888) 560-8913	Ft. Worth
Iowa, Kansas, Missouri, Nebraska	(800) 743-5323	Kansas City

Colorado, Montana, North Dakota, South Dakota, Utah, Wyoming	(800) 877-7353	Denver
American Samoa, Arizona, California, Guam, Hawaii, Nevada	(800) 347-3739	San Francisco
Alaska, Idaho, Oregon, Washington	(800) 877-0246	Seattle

Your housing discrimination Complaint will be reviewed by a fair housing specialist to determine if it alleges acts that might violate the Fair Housing Act. The specialist will contact you for any additional information needed to complete this review. If your Complaint involves a possible violation of the Fair Housing Act, the specialist will assist you in filing an official housing discrimination Complaint.

Online Civil Rights Complaint Form:

https://ocrportal.hhs.gov/ocr/cp/wizard_cp.jsf

Online Fair Housing Complaint Form:

http://portal.hud.gov/hudportal/HUD?src=/topics/housing_discrimination

Short Form:

*First Name: *Last Name:

Email: *Your Address: *City:

*State: *Zip Code: Daytime Phone No:
Evening Phone No: Best Time to Call:

Who else can we call if we cannot reach you?

*1. Contact's First Name: *Last Name:

Organization:

2. Contact's First Name:

Last Name: Organization:

*Daytime Phone No: Evening Phone No:

Best Time to Call: Daytime Phone No:

Evening Phone No: Best Time to Call:

Enter Complaint Information.

*1. What happened to you? How were you discriminated against?
For example: were you refused an opportunity to rent or buy
housing? Denied a loan? Told that housing was not available
when in fact it was? Treated differently from others seeking
housing? State briefly what happened. (4000 character limit)

2. Why do you believe you are being discriminated against? It is a
violation of the law to deny you your housing rights for any of the
following factors: - race - color - religion - sex - national origin -
familial status (families with children under 18) - disability.

For example: were you denied housing because of your race?
Were you denied a mortgage loan because of your religion? Or
turned down for an apartment because you have children? Were
you harassed because you assisted someone in obtaining their
fair housing rights? Briefly explain why you think your housing
rights were denied because of any the factors listed above. (4000
character limit)

3. Who do you believe discriminated against you? Was it a landlord, owner, bank, real estate agent, broker, company, or organization?
First Name:

Last Name:

Organization:

Address:

4. Where did the alleged act of discrimination occur? Provide the address. For example: Was it at a rental unit? Single-family home? Public or Assisted Housing? A Mobile Home? did it occur at a bank or other lending institution?
Address:

City: **State:*   *Zip:*

*5. When Did The Last Act Of Discrimination Occur?

Enter the date: mm-dd-yyyy:

Is the alleged discrimination continuous or on going?
Yes No

Your housing discrimination Complaint will be reviewed by a fair housing specialist to determine if it alleges acts that might violate the Fair Housing Act. The specialist will contact you for any additional information needed to complete this review. If your Complaint involves a possible violation of the Fair Housing Act, the specialist will assist you in filing an official housing discrimination Complaint. U.S. Department of Housing and Urban Development 451 7th Street S.W., Washington, DC 20410 Telephone: (800) 669-9777 TTY: (800) 927-9275. HUD

Mental Health and Substance Abuse Services

For current information, or if you are a provider inquiring about certification processes or updates to a specific listing, call the ODMHSAS Certification Division at 405-522-3800.

A/D = Alcohol and Drug Treatment
OP MH = Outpatient Mental Health
Opd = Opioid Substitution Treatment
CMHC = Community Mental Health Center
PACT = Programs of Assertive Community Treatment
CBSCC = Community-Based Structured Crisis Centers
Gamb = Gambling Treatment
Eating = Eating Disorders Treatment
Res = Community Residential Mental Health Facilities
CCARC = Comprehensive Community Addiction Recovery Centers
PACT = Programs of Assertive Community Treatment CBSCC = Community-Based Structured Crisis Centers Gamb = Gambling Treatment
Eating = Eating Disorders Treatment
Res = Community Residential Mental Health Facilities
CCARC = Comprehensive Community Addiction Recovery Centers

Adair County Mental Health Services, L.L.C.	OP MH	Adair	Adol. & Adult Females & Males	Stilwell	(918) 207-9518
Carla Worley, P.L.L.C. dba Carla's Counseling Services	OP MH	Adair	Adol. & Adult Females & Males	Stilwell	(918) 696-2181
Fundamentals Counseling Services, L.L.C.	OP MH	Adair	Adol. & Adult Females & Males	Colcord	(479) 228-1120

Lake Francis Residential Care Home, L.L.C.	RES	Adair	Adult Females & Males	Welling	(918) 422-9907
CCA Properties of America, L.L.C. dba North Fork Correctional Facility	A/D	Beckham	Adult Males	Sayre	(580) 928-8200
Hearts of Hope, L.L.C.	A/D	Beckham	Adol. & Adult Females & Males	Piedmont	(405) 318-6593
Southern Oklahoma Treatment Services, Inc. (Mead)	A/D	Bryan	Adol. & Adult Females & Males	Mead	(580) 745-9083
Woodwater Counseling, L.L.C.	OP MH	Bryan	Adol. & Adult Females & Males	Durant	(580) 745-5707
Youth Services of Bryan County, Inc.	OP MH	Bryan	Adol. Females & Males	Durant	(580) 924-6263
Center for Psychological Development, Inc.	OP MH	Bryan, Atoka	Adol. & Adult Females & Males	Durant	(580) 920-2069
Providence Service Corporation of Oklahoma	OP MH	Bryan, Marshall	Adol. & Adult Females & Males	Durant	(580) 924-6363
Gary E. Miller Canadian Co. Children's Justice Center	A/D	Canadian	Adol. & Adult Females & Males	El Reno	(405) 262-0202

Shepherd Manor Residential Care, Inc.	RES	Canadian	Adult Females & Males	Oklahoma City	(405) 262-2440
Youth and Family Services, Inc.	A/D	Canadian	Adol. Females & Males	El Reno	(405) 262-6555
Arbuckle Life Solutions, Inc.	A/D	Carter	Adult Females & Males	Ardmore	(580) 226-1656
Mental Health Services of Southern Oklahoma, Inc.	A/D	Carter	Adult Females & Males	Ardmore	(580) 223-5070
Mental Health Services of Southern Oklahoma, Inc.	CBSCC	Carter	Adult Females & Males	Ardmore	(580) 798-4523
Southern Oklahoma Treatment Services, Inc. (Ardmore)	A/D	Carter	Adol. & Adult Females & Males	Mead	(580) 226-5003
Southern Oklahoma Treatment Services, Inc. (Mead & Ardmore)	Opd	Carter; Marshall	Adult Females & Males	Mead	(580) 745-9083
Mental Health Services of Southern Oklahoma, Inc.	CMHC	Carter; Pontotoc; Bryan; Garvin; Seminole; Johnston; Oklahoma		Ardmore	(580) 223-5070

Calming Connections, L.L.C.	OP MH	Cherokee	Adol. & Adult Females & Males	Tahlequah	(918) 453-1108
Jack Brown Treatment Center	A/D	Cherokee	Adol. Females & Males	Tahlequah	(918) 453-5519
Sugar Mountain Retreat, Inc.	RES	Cherokee	Adult Females & Males	Welling	(918) 456-1010
Creoks Mental Health Services, Inc. (Tahlequah & Wagoner)	A/D	Cherokee; Wagoner; Muskogee	Adol.& Adut Females & Males	Okmulgee	(918) 756-9411
Healing Hearts Counseling Center, L.L.C.	OP MH	Choctaw	Adol. & Adult Females & Males	Hugo	(580) 326-5279
Cornerstone Counseling Services, L.L.C.	OP MH	Choctaw; Pittsburg	Adol & Adult Females & Males	Hugo	(580-326-2200)
Center for Children and Families, Inc.	OP MH	Cleveland	Adol. & Adult Females & Males	Norman	(405) 364-1420
Central Okla. CMHC	CMHC	Cleveland		Norman	(405) 360-5100
Central Okla. CMHC	PACT	Cleveland		Norman	(405) 360-5100
Children's Recovery Center of Oklahoma	A/D	Cleveland	Adolescent Females & Males	Norman	(405) 364-9004
Children's Recovery Center of Oklahoma	CBSCC	Cleveland	Adolescent	Norman	(405) 364-9004

Communitywo rks, L.L.C.	A/D	Cleveland	Adol. & Adult Females & Males	Norman	(405) 447-4499
Creating Options, L.L.C.	OP MH	Cleveland	Adol. & Adult Females & Males	Norman	(405) 217-4547
High Cedar Residential Care	RES	Cleveland	Adult Females & Males	Noble	(405) 447-2532
Journey Therapeutic Services, P.L.L.C.	OP MH	Cleveland	Adults Females & Males	Norman	(580) 559-2347
Living Hope Eating Disorder Treatment Center, P.L.L.C.	Eatin g	Cleveland		Norman	(405) 801-2323
Moore Youth and Family Services, Inc.	A/D	Cleveland	Adol. & Adult Females & Males	Moore	(405) 799-7761
Moore Youth and Family Services, Inc.	OP MH	Cleveland	Adol. & Adult Females & Males	Moore	(405) 799-3379
NCC Partners, L.L.C. dba Norman Counseling Clinic	OP MH	Cleveland	Adol. & Adult Females & Males	Norman	(405) 360-0556
Norman Addiction Information & Counseling, Inc.dba NAIC	Gamb	Cleveland		Norman	(405) 321-0022
Okla. MH Council, Inc. dba Red Rock	CBSC C	Cleveland	Adults	Oklaho ma City	(405) 307-4800

BHS (Norman-GMH)					
Okla. MH Council, Inc. dba Red Rock BHS (Norman-NRH)	CBSC C	Cleveland	Adults	Oklaho ma City	(405) 307-4800
Norman Addiction Information & Counseling, Inc.dba NAIC	A/D	Cleveland; McClain	Adol. & Adult Females & Males	Norman	(405) 321-0022
Center for Psychological Development, Inc.	OP MH	Coal, Pittsburg, Latimer	Adol. & Adult Females & Males	Durant	(580) 920-2069
Hope Family Clinic, P.L.L.C.	OP MH	Comanche	Adol. & Adult Females & Males	Lawton	(580) 357-3857
Hope Family Clinic, P.L.L.C.	A/D	Comanche	Adol & Adult Females & Males	Lawton	(580) 357-3857
Jim Taliaferro CMHC (Res) (Bridges to Recovery)	A/D	Comanche	Adult Females	Lawton	(580) 248-5780
Jim Taliaferro CMHC (OP)	A/D	Comanche	Adult Females & Males	Lawton	(580) 248-5780
Jim Taliaferro CMHC	PACT	Comanche		Lawton	(580) 248-5436
Jim Taliaferro CMHC	Gamb	Comanche		Lawton	(580) 355-0072
Life Management Counseling & Consulting, Inc.	A/D	Comanche	Adult Females & Males	Lawton	(580) 351-1188

Premier Behavioral Health Counseling, L.L.C.	A/D	Comanche	Adol. & Adult Females & Males	Lawton	(580) 699-8551
Premier Behavioral Health Counseling, L.L.C.	OP MH	Comanche	Adol. & Adult Females & Males	Lawton	(580) 699-8551
Roadback, Inc.	A/D	Comanche	Adol. & Adult Females & Males	Lawton	(580) 357-8114
Roadback, Inc.	CCARC	Comanche	Adult Females & Males	Lawton	(580) 357-8114
Southern Oklahoma Treatment Services, Inc. (Lawton)	Opd	Comanche	Adult Females & Males	Mead	(580) 355-7500
Multi-County Counseling, Inc. (Lawton)	A/D	Comanche; Beckham	Adol. & Adult Females & Males	Purcell	(580) 581-1818
Jim Taliaferro CMHC	CMHC	Comanche; Stephens; Jackson; Caddo		Lawton	(580) 248-5780
Edna Lee's Room & Board, Inc. dba Edna Lee's Residential Care	RES	Craig	Adult Females & Males	Vinita	(918) 256-3131
Homestead Residential Care, L.L.C.	RES	Craig	Adult Females & Males	Vinita	(918) 782-9969

Miller's Residential Care, L.L.C.	RES	Craig	Adult Females & Males	Vinita	(918) 256-3796
Orchard Grove Residential Care Facility	RES	Craig	Adult Males	Vinita	(918) 782-4184
Rose Rock Recovery Center	A/D	Craig	Adult Females	Vinita	(918) 256-9210
Santa Fe Residential Care Home, L.L.C.	RES	Craig	Adult Males	Vinita	(918) 256-3424
TAD Investments, L.L.C. dba Rambling Rose Independent Living	RES	Craig	Adult Females & Males	Langley	(918) 782-9370
Transcendence, L.L.C.	OP MH	Craig	Adol. & Adult Females & Males	Vinita	(918) 915-0084
ROCMND Area Youth Services, Inc.	A/D	Craig; Delaware; Mayes	Adol. Females & Males	Vinita	(918) 256-7518
ROCMND Area Youth Services, Inc.	OP MH	Craig; Delaware; Mayes; Ottawa	Adol. & Adult Females & Males	Vinita	(918) 256-7518
Creoks Mental Health Services, Inc. (Spring Creek Clinic)	CBSC C	Creek		Okmulgee	(918) 227-2016
Tulsa Boys' Home, Inc.	A/D	Creek	Adol. Males	Tulsa	(918) 245-0231

Creeks Mental Health Services, Inc.	CMHC	Creek; Okmulgee; Okfuskee; Cherokee; Wagoner; Sequoyah; Adair		Okmulg ee	(918) 756-9411
Hearts of Hope, L.L.C. (Elk City)	OP MH	Custer	Adol. & Adult Females & Males	Piedmo nt	(405) 318-6593
Okla. MH Council, Inc. dba Red Rock BHS (Clinton)	CBSC C	Custer	Adults	Oklaho ma City	(580) 323-6021
House of Hope, Inc.	A/D	Delaware	Adult Females & Males (res-males)	Grove	(918) 787-2242
YCO OKC, Inc. (Grove)	OP MH	Delaware; Mayes; Ottawa	Adol. & Adult Females & Males	Grove	(918) 791-9700
Associated Therapeutic Services, P.C.	A/D	Garfield	Adol. & Adult Females & Males	Enid	(580) 242-4673
Youth and Family Services of North Central Oklahoma, Inc.	A/D	Garfield	Adol. & Adult Females & Males	Enid	(580) 233-7220
YWCA Reflections Halfway House	A/D	Garfield	Adult Females	Enid	(580) 234-7581

Jim Wallace & Associates, Inc. dba The Jetty Counseling Center	A/D	Garvin	Adol. & Adult Females & Males	Wynne wood	(405) 665-4385
Byte & Associates, L.L.C.	A/D	Grady	Adol. & Adult Females & Males	Chickas ha	(405) 222-4786
Southwest Youth and Family Services, Inc.	A/D	Grady; Caddo	Adol. & Adult Females & Males	Chickas ha	(405) 222-5437
Southwest Youth and Family Services, Inc.	Gamb	Grady; Caddo		Chickas ha	(405) 222-5437
New Hope CDU, L.L.C.	A/D	Greer; Jackson; Washita	Adult Females & Males	Mangu m	(580) 782-3337
Southwestern Youth Services, Inc.	A/D	Jackson	Adol.Fema les & Males	Altus	(580) 482-2809
Southeastern Oklahoma Family Services, Inc.	A/D	Johnston	Ado. & Adult Females & Males	Kingsto n	(580) 371-3672
Alpha II, Inc.	A/D	Kay	Adult Males	Tonkaw a	(580) 628-2539
Bridgeway, Inc.	A/D	Kay	Adol. & Adult Females & Males	Ponca City	(580) 762-1462
Bridgeway, Inc.	Gamb	Kay		Ponca City	(580) 762-1462
Edwin Fair CMHC, Inc.	PACT	Kay		Ponca City	(580) 762-7561

Edwin Fair CMHC, Inc.	CMHC	Kay; Payne; Noble; Osage		Ponca City	(580) 762-7561
Rural Intervention Services Enterprises, P.L.L.C.	A/D	Latimer, LeFlore	Adol. & Adult Females & Males	Wilburton	(918) 465-7890
Rural Intervention Services Enterprises, P.L.L.C.	OP MH	Latimer, LeFlore	Adol. & Adult Females & Males	Wilburton	(918) 465-7890
Cavanal Counseling, Inc.	A/D	LeFlore	Adol. & Adult Females & Males	Poteau	(918) 647-0485
Eastern Oklahoma Mental Health & Counseling, L.L.C.	OP MH	LeFlore	Adol. & Adult Females & Males	Poteau	(918) 649-0011
Meadow Brook Residential Facility, L.L.C.	RES	LeFlore	Adult Females & Males	Howe	(918) 658-2509
Sequoyah Counseling Services of Oklahoma, Inc.	A/D	LeFlore	Adol. & Adult Females & Males	Poteau	(918) 649-0067
Serenity Counseling, Inc.	OP MH	LeFlore	Ado. & Adult Females & Males	Cartwright	(918) 647-9629
Chase E. Inc. dba 3C Old Fashion Boarding Home	RES	Lincoln	Adult Males	Prague	(405) 567-2280

Abundant Life Today Services, L.L.C.	OP MH	Logan	Adol. & Adult Females & Males	Guthrie	(405) 340-0085
Eagle Ridge Institute, Inc. dba Eagle Ridge Family Treatment Center (Guthrie)	A/D	Logan	Adult Females	Oklahoma City	(405) 282-8232
Four Winds Ranch Recovery Center for Adolescent Females, L.L.C.	A/D	Logan	Adolescent Females	Guthrie	(405) 260-0212
Logan Community Services, Inc.	A/D	Logan	Adol. & Adult Females & Males	Guthrie	(405) 282-5524
Fair Oaks Residential Care, L.L.C.	RES	Mayes	Adult Males	Langley	(918) 782-3180
Pushmataha Counseling Services, Inc.	A/D	Mayes	Adult Females & Males	Pryor	(918) 825-4872
Creoks Mental Health Services, Inc. (Pryor and Vinita)	OP MH	Mayes; Craig	Adol. & Adult Females & Males	Okmulgee	(918) 968-4600
Carl Albert CMHC	PACT	McAlester		McAlester	(918) 426-7800
Rob's Road to Recovery Ranch, L.L.C.	A/D	McClain	Adult Males	Purcell	(405) 253-3838
Full Life Family Resource Center, L.L.C.	OP MH	McCurtain	Adol. & Adult Females & Males	Broken Bow	(580) 584-2478

Kiamichi Youth Services for McCurtain County, Inc.	OP MH	McCurtain	Adol & Adult Females & Males	Idabel	(580) 286-6671
Mental Health Center, Inc. (The)	OP MH	McCurtain	Adol. & Adult Females & Males	Idabel	(580) 286-5184
Valliant House, L.L.C.	A/D	McCurtain	Adult Females & Males	Valliant	(580) 933-7031
Kiamichi Council on Alcoholism and Other Drug Abuse, Inc.	A/D	McCurtain; Bryan; Choctaw;	Adol. & Adult Females & Males	Idabel	(580) 286-3301
Kiamichi Council on Alcoholism and Other Drug Abuse, Inc.	Gamb	McCurtain; Bryan; Choctaw;		Idabel	(580) 286-3301
Crossway Counseling Services, L.L.C.	A/D	Murray	Adol. & Adult Females & Males	Sulphur	(580) 622-6127
Crossway Counseling Services, L.L.C.	OP MH	Murray	Adol. & Adult Females & Males	Sulphur	(580) 622-6127
Green Country Behavioral Health Services, Inc.	CBSC C	Muskogee	Adults	Muskog ee	(918) 682-8407
Monarch, Inc.	A/D	Muskogee	Adult Females	Muskog ee	(918) 682-7210

Monarch, Inc.	A/D	Muskogee	Adol. & Adult Females & Males	Muskogee	(918) 463-2581
Monarch, Inc.	OP MH	Muskogee	Adol. & Adult Females & Males	Muskogee	(918) 463-2581
Muskogee Co. Council of Youth Services, Inc.	OP MH	Muskogee	Adol. & Adult Females & Males	Muskogee	(918) 682-2841
Song Byrd Behavioral Health, Inc.	OP MH	Muskogee	Adol. & Adult Females & Males	Ft. Gibson	(918) 681-4201
Green Country Behavioral Health Services, Inc.	CMHC	Muskogee; McIntosh		Muskogee	(918) 682-8407
Muskogee Co. Council of Youth Services, Inc.	A/D	Muskogee; Wagoner	Adol. & Adult Females & Males	Muskogee	(918) 682-2841
Grand Lake Mental Health Center, Inc.	CMHC	Nowata; Ottawa; Washington; Rogers; Delaware; Mayes; Craig; Oklahoma		Nowata	(918) 273-1841
Spears Management Co., Inc. dba Boley Residential Care Home I	RES	Okfuskee	Adult Females & Males	Boley	(918) 667-3778

Spears Management Co., Inc. dba Boley Residential Care Home II	RES	Okfuskee	Adult Females & Males	Boley	(918) 667-3779
Spears Management Co., Inc. dba Firm Foundation Residential Care Home	RES	Okfuskee	Adult Females & Males	Boley	(918) 667-3388
Tiger Mountain Recovery, Inc.	A/D	Okfuskee	Adult Females	Henryet ta	(918) 650-9292
Creoks Mental Health Services, Inc. (Okemah)	A/D	Okfuskee; Pittsburg; Atoka	Adult Males	Okmulg ee	(918) 756-9411
3 Dimensions Counseling Services, L.L.C.	OP MH	Oklahoma	Adol. & Adult Females & Males	Edmon d	(405) 414-1088
A Better Choice-Counseling Services, L.L.C.	A/D	Oklahoma	Adult Females & Males	Oklaho ma City	(405) 604-3324
A Bright Tomorrow Counseling Services, Inc.	OP MH	Oklahoma	Adol. & Adult Females & Males	Oklaho ma City	(405) 608-6878
Access2 Counseling Services, P.L.L.C.	A/D	Oklahoma	Adol. & Adult Females & Males	Oklaho ma City	(405) 242-2242
A Chance to Change Foundation	A/D	Oklahoma	Adol. & Adult Females & Males	Oklaho ma City	(405) 840-9000

A Chance to Change Foundation	Gamb	Oklahoma		Oklahoma City	(405) 840-9000
Affinity Counseling Services, L.L.C.	OP MH	Oklahoma	Chld., Adol.& Adult Female & Males	Oklahoma City	(405) 582-2929
Alcohol Training & Education, Inc.	A/D	Oklahoma	Adult Females & Males	Oklahoma City	(405) 943-7483
An Inward Bound Family Counseling Center, L.L.C.	OP MH	Oklahoma	Adol. & Adult Females & Males	Oklahoma City	(405) 516-0343
Another Chance Counseling Agency, Inc.	A/D	Oklahoma	Adol. & Adult Females & Males	Midwest City	(405) 778-8007
Another Chance Counseling Agency, Inc.	OP MH	Oklahoma	Adol. & Adult Females & Males	Midwest City	(405) 778-8007
Aurora Counseling Services, Inc.	A/D	Oklahoma	Adol. & Adult Females & Males	Oklahoma City	(405) 634-4434
Beacon Pointe, L.L.C.	A/D	Oklahoma	Adol. & Adult Females & Males	Oklahoma City	(405) 848-5620
Carver Transitional Center, L.L.C.	A/D	Oklahoma	Adult Females & Males	Oklahoma City	(405) 232-8233
Center for Wholly Living, L.L.C.	OP MH	Oklahoma	Adol. & Adult Females & Males	Oklahoma City	(405) 706-5971

Center Point, Inc. (OKC)	A/D	Oklahoma	Adult Males	Oklaho ma City	(405) 605-2491
Clear View Professional Counseling, Inc.	OP MH	Oklahoma	Adol. & Adult Females & Males	Oklaho ma City	(405) 848-2310
Community Adolescent Rehabilitation Effort (Care) for Change, Inc.	A/D	Oklahoma	Adol. & Adult Females & Males	Oklaho ma City	(405) 524-5525
Community Adolescent Rehabilitation Effort (Care) for Change, Inc.	OP MH	Oklahoma	Adol & Adult Females & Males	Oklaho ma City	(405) 524-5525
Concepts in Counseling, L.L.C.	A/D	Oklahoma	Adol. & Adult Females & Males	Oklaho ma City	(405) 702-9032
COPE, Inc.	CCAR C	Oklahoma	Adult Females & Males	Oklaho ma City	(405) 528-8686
Cornerstone Counseling & Consulting, Inc.	A/D	Oklahoma	Adol. & Adult Females & Males	Oklaho ma City	(405) 231-3150
Cornerstone Counseling & Consulting, Inc.	OP MH	Oklahoma	Adol. & Adult Females & Males	Oklaho ma City	(405) 231-3150
Counseling Solutions & Interventions, Inc.	A/D	Oklahoma	Adol. & Adult Females & Males	Oklaho ma City	(405) 601-6710
Counseling Solutions & Interventions, Inc.	OP MH	Oklahoma	Adol. & Adult Females & Males	Oklaho ma City	(405) 601-6710

Dallas Restorative Family Services, Inc.	OP MH	Oklahoma	Adol. & Adult Females & Males	Edmond	(405) 245-7590
Drug Recovery, Inc. dba Catalyst Behavioral Services	A/D	Oklahoma	Adult Females & Males	Oklahoma City	(405) 232-9804
Drug Recovery, Inc. dba Catalyst Behavioral Services	CCARC	Oklahoma	Adult Females & Males	Oklahoma City	(405) 232-9804
Edmond Family Counseling, Inc.	A/D	Oklahoma	Adol. & Adult Females & Males	Edmond	(405) 341-3554
Family & Children's Consultants, Inc.	OP MH	Oklahoma	Adol. & Adult Females & Males	Oklahoma City	(405) 943-7500
Family Development and Intervention Services, Inc.	A/D	Oklahoma	Adol. & Adult Females & Males	Oklahoma City	(405) 767-1126
Family Directions Behavioral Health Services, L.L.C.	OP MH	Oklahoma	Adol. & Adult Females & Males	Oklahoma City	(405) 604-6857
Family Recovery, Inc. dba Family Recovery Counseling Center	A/D	Oklahoma	Adult Females & Males	Oklahoma City	(405) 524-2424
Family Recovery, Inc. dba Family Recovery	OP MH	Oklahoma	Adol. & Adult Females & Males	Oklahoma City	(405) 524-2424

Counseling Center					
Full Function Rehabilitation, P.L.L.C.	OP MH	Oklahoma	Adol. & Adult Females & Males	Oklahoma City	(405) 634-1111
Hav-Tap, Inc. dba The Harbor	RES	Oklahoma	Adult Females & Males	Oklahoma City	(405) 943-2273
Healthy Life Interventions, L.L.C.	OP MH	Oklahoma	Adol. & Adult Females & Males	Edmond	(405) 285-7019
Hearts of Hope, L.L.C. (Edmond)	OP MH	Oklahoma	Adol. & Adult Females & Males	Piedmont	(405) 318-6593
Helping Hands Making Brighter Futures, L.L.C.	OP MH	Oklahoma	Adol. & Adult Females & Males	Oklahoma City	(405) 470-8778
Hope Community Services, Inc.	CMHC	Oklahoma		Oklahoma City	(405) 634-4400
iAspire Family Services, Inc.	OP MH	Oklahoma	Adult, Adol. Females & Males & Child	Oklahoma City	(405)543-2603
LaNai P, P.C. dba Spring Eternal	OP MH	Oklahoma	Adol. & Adult Females & Males	Oklahoma City	(405) 601-4565
Latino Community Development Agency, Inc.	A/D	Oklahoma	Adol. & Adult Females & Males	Oklahoma City	(405) 236-0701

Lifeline Mental Health Services, Inc.	OP MH	Oklahoma	Adol. & Adult Females & Males	Edmond	(405) 285-2080
Maximus Counseling, Inc.	A/D	Oklahoma	Adol. & Adult Females & Males	Oklahoma City	(405) 601-1154
Mid-Del Youth & Family Center, Inc.	A/D	Oklahoma	Adol. Females & Males	Midwest City	(405) 733-5437
Mission Treatment Centers, Inc. (OKC)	Opd	Oklahoma	Adult Females & Males	Las Vegas	(405) 239-6815
Mi-Win, Inc. dba Justin's Lighthouse Recovery Services (OKC)	OP MH	Oklahoma	Adol. & Adult Females & Males	Tulsa	(405) 919-8781
MMLD, Inc. dba New Beginnings Counseling Services	A/D	Oklahoma	Adol. & Adult Females & Males	Oklahoma City	(405) 842-0500
Mosaic Mental Health, L.L.C.	OP MH	Oklahoma	Adol. & Adult Females & Males	Oklahoma City	(405) 595-9600
New Alternatives Center, L.L.C.	A/D	Oklahoma	Adult Females & Males	Oklahoma City	(405) 601-4669
New Day Recovery Youth & Family Services, Inc.	A/D	Oklahoma	Adult Females & Males	Oklahoma City	(405) 525-0452
New Discoveries Youth and	A/D	Oklahoma	Adol. & Adult Females & Males	Oklahoma City	(405) 232-1401

Family Services, Inc.					
North Okla. Co. MH Center, Inc. dba Northcare	PACT	Oklahoma		Oklaho ma City	(405) 858-2700
Oklahoma Brain Tumor Foundation	OP MH	Oklahoma	Adol. & Adult Females & Males	Oklaho ma City	(405) 843-4673
Oklahoma Counseling and Intervention Center, L.L.C.	OP MH	Oklahoma	Adult Females & Males	Oklaho ma City	(405) 753-7159
Oklahoma County Crisis Intervention Center	CBSC C	Oklahoma	Adults	Oklaho ma City	(405) 522-8100
Oklahoma Crisis Recovery Unit	CBSC C	Oklahoma	Adults	Oklaho ma City	(405) 522-8168
Okla. MH Council, Inc. dba Red Rock BHS (Okla. City)	PACT	Oklahoma		Oklaho ma City	(405) 425-0341
Okla. MH Council, Inc. dba Red Rock BHS (Jordan's Crossing)	A/D	Oklahoma	Adult Females	Oklaho ma City	(405) 425-0355
Okla. MH Council, Inc. dba Red Rock BHS (Okla. City)	CBSC C	Oklahoma	Children and Youth	Oklaho ma City	(405) 424-7711

Oklahoma Treatment Services, L.L.C. dba Rightway Medical	Opd	Oklahoma	Adult Females & Males	Oklaho ma City	(405) 616-3366
Open Options, Inc.	A/D	Oklahoma	Adol. & Adult Females & Males	Oklaho ma City	(405) 557-1655
Pathways Professional Counseling, Inc.	A/D	Oklahoma	Adult Females & Males	Oklaho ma City	(405) 842-7284
Prevention Center, L.L.C. (The)	OP MH	Oklahoma	Adol. & Adult Females & Males	Oklaho ma City	(405) 835-6757
Primary Therapeutic Services, R.L.L.P.	OP MH	Oklahoma	Adol. & Adult Females & Males	Oklaho ma City	(405) 607-6292
Promises, Inc.	A/D	Oklahoma	Adol. & Adult Females & Males	Oklaho ma City	(405) 270-0005
Promises, Inc.	Gamb	Oklahoma		Oklaho ma City	(405) 270-0005
Promises, Inc.	OP MH	Oklahoma	Adol. & Adult Females & Males	Oklaho ma City	(405) 270-0005
Reach for the Light, Inc. dba The Enrichment Center	A/D	Oklahoma	Adol. & Adult Females & Males	Oklaho ma City	(405) 601-0295
Referral Center for Alcohol and Drug Services	A/D	Oklahoma	Adult Females & Males	Oklaho ma City	(405) 525-2525

of Central Okla., Inc. (The)					
Referral Center for Alcohol and Drug Services of Central Okla., Inc. (The)	CCAR C	Oklahoma	Adol. & Adult Females & Males	Oklaho ma City	(405) 525-2525
Roberts & Co., Inc. dba Group Counseling	OP MH	Oklahoma	Adol. & Adult Females & Males	Edmon d	(405) 474-5359
Southern Oklahoma Treatment Services, Inc. (OKC)	Opd	Oklahoma	Adult Females & Males	Oklaho ma City	(405) 942-7650
Specialized Outpatient Services, Inc.	A/D	Oklahoma	Adol. & Adult Females & Males	Oklaho ma City	(405) 810-1766
T. Greene Management, L.L.C.	OP MH	Oklahoma	Adol. & Adult Females & Males	Edmon d	(405) 285-7019
Total Life Counseling Foundation	A/D	Oklahoma	Adult Females & Males	Oklaho ma City	(405) 840-7040
Total Life Counseling Foundation	OP MH	Oklahoma	Adol. & Adult Females & Males	Oklaho ma City	(405) 840-7040
Tri-City Youth and Family Center, Inc.	A/D	Oklahoma	Adol. & Adult Females & Males	Chocta w	(405) 390-8131

Tri-City Youth and Family Center, Inc.	OP MH	Oklahoma	Adol. & Adult Females & Males	Choctaw	(405) 390-8131
Valley Hope Assoc. dba Oklahoma City Valley Hope	A/D	Oklahoma	Adult Females & Males	Norton	(405) 946-7337
VCPHCS IV, L.L.C. dba New Beginnings Medical Center	Opd	Oklahoma	Adult Females & Males	Dallas	(405) 681-2003
Y.C.O. Clinton, Inc. (Oklahoma City)	A/D	Oklahoma	Adol. & Adult Females & Males	Oklahoma City	(405) 200-0181
Your Key to Change, L.L.C.	A/D	Oklahoma	Adol. & Adult Females & Males	Oklahoma City	(405) 414-2301
Your Key to Change, L.L.C.	OP MH	Oklahoma	Adol. & Adult Females & Males	Oklahoma City	(405) 414-2301
Youth Services for Okla. Co., Inc.	A/D	Oklahoma	Adol. & Adult Females & Males	Oklahoma City	(405) 235-7537
Community Action Agency of Ok. & Canadian Counties dba Turning Point	A/D	Oklahoma; Canadian	Adult Females & Males	Oklahoma City	(405) 232-0199

YCO OKC, Inc.	OP MH	Oklahoma; Kingfisher; Canadian	Adol. & Adult Females & Males	Oklaho ma City	(405) 200-0126
North Okla. Co. MH Center, Inc. dba Northcare	CMH C	Oklahoma; Logan		Oklaho ma City	(405) 858-2700
COPE, Inc.	A/D	Oklahoma; Pottawato mie	Adult Females & Males	Oklaho ma City	(405) 528-8686
Muscogee (Creek) Nation Behavioral Health & SA Services	A/D	Okmulgee; Creek; Okfuskee; McIntosh; Wagoner	Adol. & Adult Females & Males	Okmulg ee	(918) 758-1910
Keystone Counseling and Therapeutic Services, L.L.C.	OP MH	Osage	Adol. & Adult Females & Males	Clevela nd	(918) 358-5339
Osage Nation Counseling Center	A/D	Osage	Adult Females & Males	Pawhus ka	(918) 287-5466
Intertribal Council, Inc. dba Inter-Tribal SA/Prevention & Treatment Center	A/D	Ottawa	Adult Females & Males	Miami	(918) 542-5543
Life Management, Inc.	OP MH	Ottawa	Ado. & Adult Females & Males	Afton	(918) 257-9570
Quapaw Counseling Services	Opd	Ottawa	Adult Females & Males	Miami	(918) 542-1786

Northeastern Oklahoma Council on Alcoholism, Inc.	A/D	Ottawa; Delaware; Craig	Adol. & Adult Females & Males	Miami	(918) 675-4100
United Community Action Program, Inc. dba Community Alcoholism Services	A/D	Pawnee	Adult Females & Males	Pawnee	(918) 762-3041
Edwin Fair CMHC, Inc.	PACT	Payne		Ponca City	(58) 762-7561
Payne Co. Drug Court, Inc.	A/D	Payne	Adol. & Adult Females & Males	Stillwater	(405) 743-1968
Payne Co. Youth Services, Inc.	A/D	Payne	Adol.Females & Males	Stillwater	(405) 377-3380
Valley Hope Assoc. dba Cushing Valley Hope	A/D	Payne	Adult Females & Males	Norton	(918) 225-1736
Creeks Mental Health Services, Inc. (Stroud)	OP MH	Payne; Pottawatomie; Creek; Oklahoma	Adol. & Adult Females & Males	Okmulgee	(918) 968-4600
Community Counselors Group, Inc.	OP MH	Pittsburg	Adol. & Adult Females & Males	Hartshorne	(918) 297-3400
Dow Residential Care Facility, Inc.	RES	Pittsburg	Adult Females & Males	Hartshorne	(918) 297-2485

Narconon of Oklahoma, Inc. dba Narconon Arrowhead	A/D	Pittsburg	Adult Females & Males	Canadia n	(918) 339-5761
Phoenix Gate, Inc.	A/D	Pittsburg	Adult Females & Males	Hartsho rne?	(918) 423-9400
Phoenix Gate, Inc.	OP MH	Pittsburg	Adol. & Adult Females & Males	Hartsho rne	(918) 423-9400
Professional Counseling and Consulting Services, P.C.	A/D	Pittsburg	Adol. & Adult Females & Males	McAlest er	(918) 420-5238
Professional Counseling and Consulting Services, P.C.	OP MH	Pittsburg	Adol. & Adult Females & Males	McAlest er	(918) 420-5238
Southeastern Oklahoma Social Services, Inc.	A/D	Pittsburg	Adol. & Adult Females & Males	McAlest er	(918) 302-0389
Carl Albert CMHC	CMH C	Pittsburg; Hughes; LeFlore; Choctaw; McCurtain; Haskell; Atoka		McAlest er	(918) 426-7800
Ki Bois Comm. Action Found., Inc. dba The Oaks Rehab. Services Center	A/D	Pittsburg; LeFlore; McIntosh; Haskell; Latimer	Adol. & Adult Females & Males	Stigler	(918) 967-3325

Area Youth Shelter, Inc.	A/D	Pontotoc	Adol. & Adult Females & Males	Ada	(580) 436-6130
Area Youth Shelter, Inc.	OP MH	Pontotoc	Adol. & Adult Females & Males	Ada	(580) 436-6130
Biofeedback Solutions, L.L.C.	OP MH	Pontotoc	Adol. & Adult Females & Males	Ada	(580) 453-1835
Carl Albert CMHC	PACT	Pontotoc		McAlester	(580) 332-3699
Chickasaw Nation Healthy Lifestyles	A/D	Pontotoc	Adult Females & Males	Ada	(580) 332-6345
Providence Service Corporation of Oklahoma	OP MH	Pontotoc	Adol. & Adult Females & Males	Durant	(580) 332-6851
Addiction & Behavioral Health Center, Inc.	A/D	Pontotoc; Seminole	Adol. & Adult Females & Males	Ada	(580) 332-3001
Athena Rehabilitation Services, L.L.C. dba VizOwn	A/D	Pottawatomie	Adult Females	Tecumseh	(405) 253-2020
Focus Counseling, L.L.C.	OP MH	Pottawatomie	Adol. & Adult Females & Males	Shawnee	(405) 432-4132
H. Chandler & Associates, L.L.C. (Shawnee)	A/D	Pottawatomie	Adol. & Adult Females & Males	Shawnee	(405) 481-7442

Hope Revealed Behavioral Health Center, L.L.C.	OP MH	Pottawato mie	Adol. & Adult Females & Males	Shawne e	(405) 596-3833
Okla. MH Council, Inc. dba Red Rock BHS (Shawnee)	PACT	Pottawato mie		Oklaho ma City	(405) 425-0355
Okla. MH Council, Inc. dba Red Rock BHS	CMH C	Pottawato mie; Lincoln; Custer; Blaine; Canadian; Oklahoma; Grady; Beckham; Kiowa; Kingfisher		Oklaho ma City	(405) 425-0355
Gateway to Prevention and Recovery, Inc.	Gamb	Pottawato mie; Payne		Shawne e	(405) 273-1170
Gateway to Prevention and Recovery, Inc.	CCAR C	Pottawato mie; Payne	Adol. & Adult Females & Males	Shawne e	(405) 273-1170
Quest MHSA, L.L.C.	A/D	Pushmatah a	Adol. & Adult Females & Males	Antlers	(580) 298-3001
Zen Gee Counseling & Psychological Services, L.L.C.	A/D	Pushmatah a	Adol. & Adult Females & Males	Antlers	(580) 298-5062

Providence Service Corporation of Oklahoma	OP MH	Pushmataha, Choctaw, McCurtain	Adol. & Adult Females & Males	Durant	(580) 326-7477
SequelCare of Oklahoma, L.L.C.	A/D	Pushmataha; LeFlore; Choctaw; McCurtain; Bryan	Adol. & Adult Females & Males	Antlers	(580) 298-2830
Community Counseling and Testing Services, L.L.C.	OP MH	Rogers	Adol. & Adult Females & Males	Claremore	(918) 923-6444
Copp's Residential Care, Inc.	RES	Rogers	Adult Females & Males	Claremore	(918) 341-2543
Human Skills and Resources, Inc. (Claremore)	A/D	Rogers	Adol. & Adult Females & Males	Tulsa	(918) 747-6377
Rogers County Drug Abuse Program, Inc.	A/D	Rogers	Adol. & Adult Females & Males	Claremore	(918) 342-3334
Rogers County Youth Services, Inc.	OP MH	Rogers	Adol. Females & Males	Claremore	(918) 341-7580
C.B.W., Inc. dba Golden Years Residential Care	RES	Seminole	Adult Females & Males	Purcell	(580) 925-3618
Clay Crossing Foundation, Inc.	A/D	Seminole	Adult Males	Maud	(405) 374-1225
Central Oklahoma Family	A/D	Seminole; Cleveland	Adult Females & Males	Konawa	(580) 925-8809

Medical Center, Inc.					
Oklahoma Families First, Inc.	A/D	Seminole; Pontotoc	Adol. & Adult Females & Males	Norman	(405) 360-2133
LeQuita J. Joyce, Inc. dba Roland Family Counseling Center	OP MH	Sequoyah	Adol. & Adult Females & Males	Roland	(918) 427-1311
Oklahoma Treatment Services, L.L.C. dba Rightway Medical of Roland	Opd	Sequoyah	Adult Females & Males	Tulsa	(918) 427-3344
Sequoyah MH Facility, Inc. dba Sequoyah Residential Facility	RES	Sequoyah	Adult Females & Males	Howe	(918) 775-7751
People, Inc. of Sequoyah County	A/D	Sequoyah; Cherokee; Adair	Adol. & Adult Females & Males	Sallisaw	(918) 775-7787
Duncan Community Residence, Inc.	RES	Stephens	Adult Females & Males	Duncan	(580) 255-8330
Gillispie Family Ministries, Inc. dba Gillispie Counseling Services	OP MH	Stephens	Adol. & Adult Females & Males	Duncan	(580) 606-6577
Serenity Recovery Solutions, Inc.	A/D	Stephens	Adult Females & Males	Durant	(580) 475-0148

Youth Services for Stephens Co., Inc.	A/D	Stephens	Adol. & Adult Females & Males	Duncan	(580) 255-8800
Youth Services for Stephens Co., Inc.	OP MH	Stephens	Adol. & Adult Females & Males	Duncan	(580) 255-8800
Professional Counseling Solutions, P.L.L.C.	A/D	Tillman	Adol. & Adult Females & Males	Frederick	(580) 335-3320
12 & 12, Inc.	A/D	Tulsa	Adult Females & Males	Tulsa	(918) 664-4224
12 & 12, Inc.	CCARC	Tulsa	Adult Females & Males	Tulsa	(918) 664-4224
Action Steps Counseling, Inc.	A/D	Tulsa	Adult Males	Tulsa	(918) 764-9098
Brighter Dimensions, L.L.C.	OP MH	Tulsa	Adol. & Adult Females & Males	Broken Arrow	(918) 280-9104
Center for Therapeutic Interventions, P.L.L.C. (The)	A/D	Tulsa	Adol. & Adult Females & Males	Tulsa	(918) 384-0002
Center for Therapeutic Interventions, P.L.L.C. (The)	CCARC	Tulsa	Adol. & Adult Females & Males	Tulsa	(918) 384-0002
Center for Therapeutic Interventions, P.L.L.C. (The)	Gamb	Tulsa		Tulsa	(918) 384-0002

Center Point, Inc. (Tulsa)	A/D	Tulsa	Adult Females	Oklahoma City	(405) 605-2491
Counseling & Recovery Services of Oklahoma, Inc. (CALM Center)	CBSCC	Tulsa	Children and Youth	Tulsa	(918) 492-2554
Counseling & Recovery Services of Oklahoma, Inc.	A/D	Tulsa	Adult Females & Males	Tulsa	(918) 492-2554
Creoks Mental Health Services, Inc. (Tulsa)	A/D	Tulsa	Adol.Females & Males	Okmulgee	(918) 382-7300
Creoks Mental Health Services, Inc. (Tulsa)	OP MH	Tulsa	Adol. & Adult Females & Males	Okmulgee	(918) 382-7300
Family and Children's Services, Inc.	A/D	Tulsa	Adult Females & Males	Tulsa	(918) 587-9471
Family and Children's Services, Inc.	CMHC	Tulsa		Tulsa	(918) 587-9471
Family and Children's Services, Inc.	CBSCC	Tulsa		Tulsa	(918) 744-4800
Family and Children's Services, Inc.	PACT	Tulsa		Tulsa	(918) 582-7228
Family and Children's Services, Inc.	Gamb	Tulsa		Tulsa	(918) 712-4301
H. Chandler & Associates, L.L.C. (Tulsa)	A/D	Tulsa	Adol. & Adult Females & Males	Tulsa	(918) 270-4660

Hahn Psyc Services, L.L.C.	OP MH	Tulsa	Adol. & Adult Females & Males	Tulsa	(918) 836-0239
Indian Health Care Resource Center of Tulsa, Inc.	A/D	Tulsa	Adult Females & Males	Tulsa	(918) 588-1900
J.A.M.E.S., Inc.	OP MH	Tulsa	Adol. & Adult Females & Males	Owasso	(918) 402-3547
Keetoowah-Cherokee Treatment Services	Opd	Tulsa	Adult Females & Males	Tulsa	(918) 835-3017
Keetoowah-Cherokee Treatment Services	A/D	Tulsa	Adult Females & Males	Tulsa	(918) 835-3017
Laureate Psychiatric Clinic and Hospital, Inc.	Eating	Tulsa		Tulsa	(918) 491-3702
Legacy Family Intervention Services, Inc.	OP MH	Tulsa	Adol. & Adult Females & Males	Tulsa	(918) 932-8591
Life Strategies International, Inc.	OP MH	Tulsa	Adol. & Adult Females & Males	Tulsa	(918) 486-9996
Love and Associates Wellness Services, P.L.L.C.	OP MH	Tulsa	Adol. & Adult Females & Males	Tulsa	(918) 794-9696
Mission Treatment Centers, Inc. (Tulsa)	Opd	Tulsa	Adult Females & Males	Las Vegas	(918) 665-2501

Mi-Win, Inc. dba Justin's Lighthouse Recovery Services (Tulsa)	OP MH	Tulsa	Adol. & Adult Females & Males	Tulsa	(918) 919-8781
North Tulsa Counseling Services, L.L.C.	OP MH	Tulsa	Adol. & Adult Females & Males	Tulsa	(918) 794-0197
Okla. MH Council, Inc. dba Red Rock BHS (Tulsa)	PACT	Tulsa		Oklahoma City	(918) 599-7404
Oklahoma Treatment Services, L.L.C. dba Tulsa Rightway Medical	Opd	Tulsa	Adult Females & Males	Tulsa	(918) 610-3366
OU Impact	PACT	Tulsa		Tulsa	(918) 660-3150
Palmer Continuum of Care, Inc.	A/D	Tulsa	Adol. & Adult Females & Males	Tulsa	(918) 430-0975
Recovery Plus Family Counseling Center, Inc.	A/D	Tulsa	Adult Females & Males	Broken Arrow	(918) 258-6900
Resonance Center For Women,Inc.	A/D	Tulsa	Adult Females	Tulsa	(918) 587-3888
Street School, Inc.	A/D	Tulsa	Adol. Females & Males	Tulsa	(918) 833-9800
Y.C.O. OKC, Inc. (Tulsa)	A/D	Tulsa	Adol. & Adult Females & Males	Oklahoma City	(918) 289-0550

YCO Tulsa, Inc.	OP MH	Tulsa	Adol. & Adult Females & Males	Oklahoma City	(918) 289-0550
Human Skills and Resources, Inc.	CCARC	Tulsa, Creek, Rogers	Adol. & Adult Females & Males	Tulsa	(918) 747-6377
Counseling & Recovery Services of Oklahoma, Inc.	CMHC	Tulsa; Creek		Tulsa	(918) 492-2554
Human Skills and Resources, Inc. (Tulsa and Sapulpa)	A/D	Tulsa; Creek	Adult Females & Males	Tulsa	(918) 747-6377
Burdine, Inc. dba New Beginning Residential Care Home	RES	Wagoner	Adult Females & Males	Red Bird	(918) 483-1425
MTF Counseling Resources, L.L.C.	OP MH	Wagoner	Adol. & Adult Females & Males	Coweta	(918) 279-6565
Oklahoma Treatment Services, L.L.C. (Bartlesville)	Opd	Washington	Adult Females & Males	Tulsa	(918) 337-6007
Wilson Psychological Associates, P.L.L.C.	OP MH	Washington	Adol. & Adult Females & Males	Bartlesville	(918) 337-6050
Youth and Family Services of Washington Co., Inc.	A/D	Washington	Adol. & Adult Females & Males	Bartlesville	(918) 335-1111

Northwestern Okla. State Univ.- Community Services Program	A/D	Woods	Adult Males	Alva	(580) 327-8517
Waynoka MH Authority dba NW SA Treatment Center	A/D	Woods	Adult Females	Waynok a	(580) 824-0674
Northwest Center for Behavioral Health, Lighthouse SA	A/D	Woodward	Adult Females & Males	Woodw ard	(580) 571-3233
Western Plains Youth and Family Services, Inc.	OP MH	Woodward	Adol. Females & Males	Woodw ard	(580) 254-5322
White Horse Ranch, L.L.C.	A/D	Woodward	Adol. Females	Moorela nd	(580) 994-5649
White Horse Ranch, L.L.C.	OP MH	Woodward	Adol. & Adult Females & Males	Moorela nd	(580) 994-5649
Northwest Center for Behavioral Health	CMH C	Woodward; Woods; Garfield; Major; Guymon		Woodw ard	(580) 571-3233

Veterans
Health Coverage for Military Veterans

TRICARE® and the Affordable Care Act

Meet your minimum essential coverage requirement under the law with TRICARE or other health care coverage options

TRICARE is a benefit established by law as the health care program for uniformed service members, retired service members, and their families. The Affordable Care Act (ACA), signed into law in 2010, was created to expand access to affordable health care coverage, lower costs, and improve quality and care coordination for all Americans.

The ACA enacted a series of reforms. Some examples of these changes include prohibiting insurance companies from denying coverage to those with preexisting conditions, eliminating lifetime limits on coverage, and providing free preventive care under all health care programs.

Although the ACA does not impact your TRICARE coverage, it could impact you in other ways:

- **If you lose TRICARE coverage for any reason** *(e.g., separate from the service, age out, or your marital status changes).* If you lose TRICARE eligibility, in some cases, you may be eligible for premium-free transitional health care coverage through the Transitional Assistance Management Program (TAMP). After the 180 days of TAMP coverage, you may qualify to purchase coverage through the Continued Health Care Benefit Program (CHCBP) for an additional 18–36 months. Depending on your status, you may also qualify to purchase TRICARE Young Adult (TYA), TRICARE Reserve Select (TRS), or TRICARE Retired Reserve (TRR) after TAMP coverage ends. If you are not eligible for TAMP, you may qualify to purchase CHCBP for 18–36 months of coverage. Both of these options are considered minimum essential coverage. You can also look for other coverage options by visiting www.healthcare.gov.

MINIMUM ESSENTIAL COVERAGE

Under the Affordable Care Act (ACA), people must have health care coverage that meets a minimum standard called minimum essential coverage; otherwise, they must qualify for an exemption. TRICARE coverage meets the minimum essential coverage requirement under the ACA. Most people who do not meet this provision of the law will be required to pay a fee for each month they do not have adequate coverage. The fee will be collected each year with federal tax returns. For more information, visit www.tricare.mil/aca. You can also find other health care coverage options at www.healthcare.gov.

- **If you qualify for TRS, TRR, TYA, or CHCBP, but you have not enrolled or have not kept up with payments.** Premium-based TRICARE or CHCBP options that require enrollment are considered minimum essential coverage under the ACA. This requirement must be met on a monthly basis and reported each year. If there are any months during which you are not enrolled or have not paid your premium, and if you did not have another form of coverage, you will **not** have met the minimum essential coverage requirement for those months. If you do not qualify or choose not to purchase a TRICARE or CHCBP premium-based program, you may find other coverage options that meet your needs at www.healthcare.gov or you can consider coverage provided by a civilian employer.

This fact sheet is not all-inclusive. For additional information, please visit www.tricare.mil.

September 2015

TRICARE PLANS

YOUR PLAN		WHAT YOU NEED TO KNOW
Considered Minimum Essential Coverage?	Yes	If you lose TRICARE eligibility (*e.g., separate from the service, age out, or your marital status changes*), you can purchase:
TRICARE Prime®		• Continued Health Care Benefit Program (CHCBP) or TRICARE Young Adult (TYA) coverage if you qualify
TRICARE Overseas Program (TOP) Prime		• Coverage from the health insurance marketplace (*www.healthcare.gov*)
TRICARE Prime Remote		• Any other plan that qualifies as minimum essential coverage (*e.g., coverage through a civilian employer or Medicare*)
TOP Prime Remote		**Note:** In some cases, you may qualify for coverage through the Transitional Assistance Management Program (TAMP).
TRICARE Prime Remote for Active Duty Family Members		
TRICARE Standard® and TRICARE Extra		
TOP Standard		
TRICARE For Life (TFL)		
TFL Overseas		
US Family Health Plan		
TRICARE Plus with TRICARE Standard		
TRICARE Plus with TFL		
Considered Minimum Essential Coverage?	Yes	Coverage is for 180 days. After the 180 days, you can purchase:
TAMP		• CHCBP or TYA coverage if you qualify
		• TRICARE Reserve Select or TRICARE Retired Reserve if you are a National Guard or Reserve member and you qualify
		• Coverage from the health insurance marketplace (*www.healthcare.gov*)
		• Any other plan that qualifies as minimum essential coverage (*e.g., coverage through a civilian employer or Medicare*)
Considered Minimum Essential Coverage?	No	If you do not have a health plan that qualifies as minimum essential coverage, you may have to pay a fee that increases every year. The fee will be collected each year with federal tax returns. To avoid paying a fee, you can purchase:
Only TRICARE Plus[1] (*not TRICARE-eligible*)		• Coverage from the health insurance marketplace (*www.healthcare.gov*)
Only direct care (*not TRICARE-eligible*)		• Any other plan that qualifies as minimum essential coverage (*e.g., coverage through a civilian employer or Medicare*)
Only line-of-duty care (*not TRICARE-eligible*)		
Only transitional care for service-related conditions[2] (*not TRICARE-eligible*)		

1. *Coverage is only for routine (primary) care at the military hospital or clinic where you are enrolled.*
2. *Coverage is only for 180 days and only for the approved condition.*

PREMIUM-BASED PLANS—YOU MUST QUALIFY FOR AND PURCHASE COVERAGE

CONTINUED HEALTH CARE BENEFIT PROGRAM

SITUATION		WHAT YOU CAN DO	WHAT YOU NEED TO KNOW
Considered Minimum Essential Coverage?	**Yes**	• Keep Continued Health Care Benefit Program (CHCBP) coverage.	You must pay your premiums on time to keep your coverage in good standing.
You qualify and purchased coverage		• Purchase coverage from the health insurance marketplace (*www.healthcare.gov*). • Purchase any other plan that qualifies as minimum essential coverage (*e.g., coverage through a civilian employer or Medicare*).	Coverage is for 18–36 months.[1] After your coverage ends, you can purchase coverage from the health insurance marketplace or any other plan that qualifies as minimum essential coverage.
Considered Minimum Essential Coverage?	**No**	• Purchase CHCBP coverage. • Purchase coverage from the health insurance marketplace (*www.healthcare.gov*).	You only have 60 days from your loss of TRICARE coverage to purchase CHCBP coverage.
You qualify but have not purchased coverage		• Purchase any other plan that qualifies as minimum essential coverage (*e.g., coverage through a civilian employer or Medicare*).	If you do not have a health plan that qualifies as minimum essential coverage, you may have to pay a fee that increases every year. The fee will be collected each year with federal tax returns.

1. *Certain former spouses who have not remarried before age 55 may qualify for an unlimited duration of coverage.*

TRICARE YOUNG ADULT

SITUATION		WHAT YOU CAN DO	WHAT YOU NEED TO KNOW
Considered Minimum Essential Coverage?	**Yes**	• Keep TRICARE Young Adult (TYA) coverage.	You must pay your premiums on time to keep your coverage in good standing.
You qualify and purchased coverage		• Purchase coverage from the health insurance marketplace (*www.healthcare.gov*). • Purchase any other plan that qualifies as minimum essential coverage (*e.g., coverage through a civilian employer or Medicare*).	After your coverage ends, you can purchase Continued Health Care Benefit Program coverage, coverage from the health insurance marketplace, or any other plan that qualifies as minimum essential coverage.
Considered Minimum Essential Coverage?	**No**	• Purchase TYA coverage. • Purchase coverage from the health insurance marketplace (*www.healthcare.gov*).	If you do not have a health plan that qualifies as minimum essential coverage, you may have to pay a fee that increases every year. The fee will be collected each year with federal tax returns.
You qualify but have not purchased coverage		• Purchase any other plan that qualifies as minimum essential coverage (*e.g., coverage through a civilian employer or Medicare*).	

More about TRICARE Young Adult

You may have heard that the Affordable Care Act extended coverage for young adult dependents (*who do not have their own insurance through an employer or spouse*) until reaching age 26. While this provision did not impact TRICARE directly, you should know that TRICARE offers coverage to qualifying young adult dependents of TRICARE sponsors through the TRICARE Young Adult (TYA) program. TYA began in 2011 and gives qualifying dependents the option to purchase premium-based TRICARE coverage until reaching age 26. For more information about whether you or family members qualify, visit www.tricare.mil/tya.

TRICARE RESERVE SELECT®

SITUATION		WHAT YOU CAN DO	WHAT YOU NEED TO KNOW
Considered Minimum Essential Coverage?	Yes	• Keep TRICARE Reserve Select (TRS) coverage.	You must pay your premiums on time to keep your coverage in good standing.
You qualify and purchased coverage		• Purchase coverage from the health insurance marketplace (*www.healthcare.gov*).	
		• Purchase any other plan that qualifies as minimum essential coverage (*e.g., coverage through a civilian employer or Medicare*).	
Considered Minimum Essential Coverage?	No	• Purchase TRS coverage.	If you do not have a health plan that qualifies as minimum essential coverage, you may have to pay a fee that increases every year. The fee will be collected each year with federal tax returns.
You qualify but have not purchased coverage		• Purchase coverage from the health insurance marketplace (*www.healthcare.gov*).	
		• Purchase any other plan that qualifies as minimum essential coverage (*e.g., coverage through a civilian employer or Medicare*).	

TRICARE RETIRED RESERVE®

SITUATION		WHAT YOU CAN DO	WHAT YOU NEED TO KNOW
Considered Minimum Essential Coverage?	Yes	• Keep TRICARE Retired Reserve (TRR) coverage.	You must pay your premiums on time to keep your coverage in good standing.
You qualify and purchased coverage		• Purchase coverage from the health insurance marketplace (*www.healthcare.gov*).	
		• Purchase any other plan that qualifies as minimum essential coverage (*e.g., coverage through a civilian employer or Medicare*).	
Considered Minimum Essential Coverage?	No	• Purchase TRR coverage.	If you do not have a health plan that qualifies as minimum essential coverage, you may have to pay a fee that increases every year. The fee will be collected each year with federal tax returns.
You qualify but have not purchased coverage		• Purchase coverage from the health insurance marketplace (*www.healthcare.gov*).	
		• Purchase any other plan that qualifies as minimum essential coverage (*e.g., coverage through a civilian employer or Medicare*).	

TAX FORM REQUIRED TO PROVE YOU HAD MINIMUM ESSENTIAL COVERAGE

For tax year 2015, an Internal Revenue Service (IRS) tax form is required to prove that you had minimum essential coverage during 2015. You will receive an IRS Form 1095 listing your TRICARE coverage status for each month in 2015. The pay center that services your military, annuity, or pension pay will provide you with your IRS Form 1095. If your military pay is administered by the Defense Finance and Accounting Services (DFAS), you can opt in to receive your 2015 IRS tax forms electronically via your DFAS myPay account. For more information and to opt-in, visit https://mypay.dfas.mil. For information about the IRS tax forms, visit www.irs.gov.

KEEP YOUR DEERS INFORMATION UP TO DATE

The IRS will collect fees from most individuals who do not maintain minimum essential coverage. TRICARE must be able to verify your coverage status based on what is listed in the Defense Enrollment Eligibility Reporting System (DEERS). You must keep your DEERS information up to date—including adding family members after marriage, birth, or adoption—in order for TRICARE to verify that all of your family members maintained minimum essential coverage. Your Social Security number (SSN) and the SSN of each of your covered family members must be included in DEERS for your TRICARE coverage to be reflected accurately.

IF YOU DO NOT HAVE MINIMUM ESSENTIAL COVERAGE FROM THE DEPARTMENT OF DEFENSE

Those who do not have minimum essential coverage from the Department of Defense can find other health care coverage options through the health insurance marketplace at www.healthcare.gov, where premium assistance or state Medicaid coverage may be available based on income, family size, and state of residence. For more information, visit www.tricare.mil/aca.

FOR INFORMATION AND ASSISTANCE

(N) TRICARE North Region	(S) TRICARE South Region	(W) TRICARE West Region
Health Net Federal Services, LLC 1-877-TRICARE (1-877-874-2273) www.hnfs.com	Humana Military, a division of Humana Government Business 1-800-444-5445 HumanaMilitary.com	UnitedHealthcare Military & Veterans 1-877-988-WEST (1-877-988-9378) www.uhcmilitarywest.com
(O) TRICARE Overseas Program (TOP) Regional Call Center—Eurasia-Africa[1] +44-20-8762-8384 (*overseas*) 1-877-678-1207 (*stateside*) tricarelon@internationalsos.com	(O) TOP Regional Call Center—Latin America and Canada[1] +1-215-942-8393 (*overseas*) 1-877-451-8659 (*stateside*) tricarephl@internationalsos.com	(O) TOP Regional Call Centers—Pacific[1] Singapore: +65-6339-2676 (*overseas*) 1-877-678-1208 (*stateside*) sin.tricare@internationalsos.com Sydney: +61-2-9273-2710 (*overseas*) 1-877-678-1209 (*stateside*) sydtricare@internationalsos.com
TRICARE Reserve Select www.tricare.mil/trs TRICARE Retired Reserve www.tricare.mil/trr	TRICARE Young Adult www.tricare.mil/tya	Transitional Assistance Management Program www.tricare.mil/tamp
Continued Health Care Benefit Program Humana Military 1-800-444-5445 www.tricare.mil/chcbp	Health Insurance Marketplace www.healthcare.gov	MilConnect Web Site (*update DEERS, get eCorrespondence*) http://milconnect.dmdc.osd.mil

1. For toll-free contact information, visit *www.tricare-overseas.com*.

If you do not have health coverage, you may have to pay a fee.

Veterans Programs That Meet Coverage Requirements:

If you're enrolled in (or are a beneficiary of) any of the programs listed below, you're considered to have minimum essential coverage under the health care law. You do not need to get additional coverage:

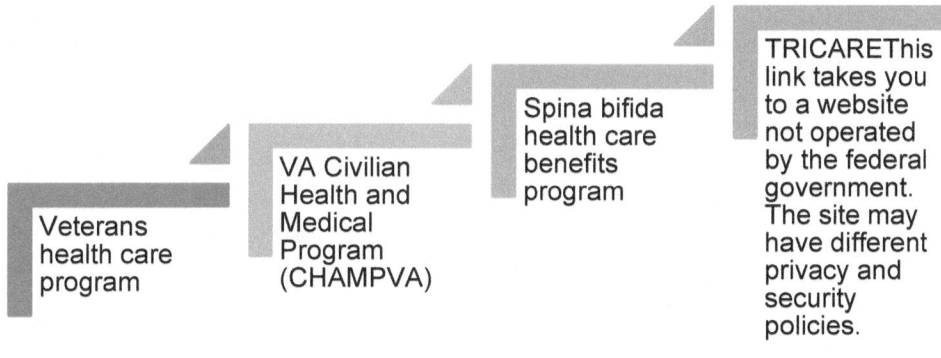

Veterans health care program

VA Civilian Health and Medical Program (CHAMPVA)

Spina bifida health care benefits program

TRICAREThis link takes you to a website not operated by the federal government. The site may have different privacy and security policies.

If You're A Veteran Without VA Health Care,

If visit the VA health care website. You may learn that you qualify for VA coverage.

For more important information on Veterans and the Affordable Care Act, visit the Department of Veterans Affairs website.

If Your Dependents Are not Covered

If you're a veteran enrolled in (or are a beneficiary of) a VA health care program, you may have dependents who are not eligible for a VA health care program. They may use the Health Insurance Marketplace to get coverage.

— Depending on household size and income, **they may get lower costs** on monthly premiums or out of pocket costs. Or they **could be eligible for free** or low-cost coverage through Medicaid or the CHIP.

— Like others, if they do not have health insurance coverage, *they may have to pay a fee.*

Note: TRICARE's young adult coverage rules are different from the Affordable Care Act's version

Homeless Vets HealthCare

Oklahoma

Muskogee (Jack C. Montgomery)

Tulsa Outpatient Clinic Attention: Mental Health

Phone Number   (918) 610-2015

Oklahoma City

HCHV Program/122H

1140 NW 32nd St.

Oklahoma. City   OK 73118

Phone Number   (405) 456-1708

Oklahoma City

HCHV Program/122H

1140 NW 32nd St.

Oklahoma. City,   OK 73118

Phone Number   (405) 456-1708

Veterans Housing Foreclosure Prevention

Are you currently at-risk of losing your housing? Are you having trouble finding or holding a job? Do you have health issues that make it difficult to work? VA is here to provide you with the support you've earned.

Call VA now at 1-877-4AID-VET (1-877-424-3838). VA can connect you with comprehensive programs—from health care to employment assistance—to prevent housing loss. Make the Call.

When you call:

- You will be connected to a trained VA responder.

- The responder will ask a few questions to assess your needs.

- If you're a Veteran, you will be connected with the Homeless Point of Contact at the nearest VA facility.

- Contact information will be requested so staff may follow up.

- 24/7 Confidential Support is a Call Away.

The Homeless Veterans hotline and online chat are free—and you do not have to be registered with VA or enrolled in VA health care. Through 1-877-4AID-VET, VA gets Veterans and their families help with:

Veterans Employment Service Representatives (LVER)
Disabled Veterans Outreach Program Specialists (DVOP)

* =Veterans' Rep available on Appointment Days

Bartlesville
210 NE Washington
Blvd
Phone (918) 332-4800
FAX (918) 332-3610
LVER: Michael
Costello
Counties Served:
Nowata, Washington
and Osage

*Claremore1810 N
Sioux Ave
 Phone (918) 341-6633
FAX (918) 341-7723
LVER: By Appointment
County Served: Rogers

*Duncan
1927 W Elk Ave
Phone (580) 255-8950
FAX (580) 255-8959
LVER: By Appointment
Counties Served:
Jefferson and
Stephens

Enid
900 W Cherokee
73701
Phone (580) 234-6043
FAX (580) 234-8405
LVER: Linda Turner

Counties Lawton
1711 SW 11th St
73501
Phone (580) 357-3500
 FAX (580) 357-9629

LVER: Robert Phillips
DVOP: Kim Burney
DVOP: OPEN apply
http://www.ok.gov/oesc
_web/
Countie Served:
Comanche, Cotton and
Tillman

McAlester 1414 E
Wade Watts Ave
74501
Phone (918) 423-6830
FAX (918) 421-6333
LVER: David Sampson
Counties Served:
Haskell, Latimer and
Pittsburg

Miami 121 N. Main
74354
Phone (918) 542-5561
FAX (918) 542-7505
LVER: Gary Rhodes
Counties Served:
Delaware and Ottawa

Muskogee 717 South
32nd Street 74401
Phone (918) 682-3364
FAX (918) 682-4311
LVER: Ryan Davis
DVOP: Daniel Reid
Counties Served:
McIntosh, Muskogee
and Wagoner

Oklahoma City
Norman 1141 E Main
St 73071
Phone (405) 701-2057
FAX (405) 701-2042
LVER: James
Mosshammer
County Served:
Cleveland

Counties Served:
Logan, Oklahoma and
Canadian
Brookwood South 9210
S Western, Ste A-9
73139 Phone (405)
234-5000 FAX (405)
378-3223
LVER: Robert Duwell
LVER: Mike Robertus
DVOP: OPEN apply
http://www.ok.gov/oesc
_web/
DVOP: Reshawnda
Morris

Eastside 7401 NE 23rd
Phone (405) 713-1890
FAX (405) 713-1882
LVER: Bill Jobe
LVER: OPEN apply
http://www.ok.gov/oesc
_web/
DVOP: OPEN apply
http://www.ok.gov/oesc
_web/

OKC VA Medical
Center 921 NE 13th St
(405) 456-5031
FAX (405) 456-1704
DVOP: Don McDaniels

Okmulgee 1801 E 4th
St
Phone (918) 756-5791
FAX (918) 756-0937
LVER: Todd
Stringfellow
County Served:
Okmulgee
Ponca City

1201 W Grand Ave
74601
Phone (580) 765-3372
FAX (580) 765-6145
LVER: Randall Coon
Counties Served: Kay,
Noble and Osage

Poteau
106 Rogers Ave 74953
Phone (918) 647-3124
FAX (918) 647-8939
LVER: William Bennett
County Served:
LeFlore
Pryor

219 NE 1st St 74361
Phone (918) 825-2582
FAX (918) 825-6494
LVER: Jack James
Counties Served: Craig
and Mayes

*Sallisaw
401 W Houser, Bldg B
74955
Phone (918) 775-5541
FAX (918) 775-6385
LVER: By Appointment
County Served:
Sequoyah

Sapulpa
1700 S. Main St 74066
Phone (918) 224-9430
FAX (918) 227-2859
LVER: Robert Williams
County Served: Creek

*Seminole
229 N 2nd St 74868
Phone (405) 382-4670
FAX (405) 382-0104
County Served:
Seminole
Shawnee

2 John C Bruton Blvd
74804
Phone (405) 275-7800
FAX (405) 878-9742
LVER: Darrell Toquitto
Counties Served:
Lincoln, Pottawatomie,
Seminole and Hughes

Stillwater
3006 E 6th St Hwy 51
74074
Phone (405) 624-1450
FAX (405) 372-0295
LVER: Bobby Bryant

County Served: Payne

*Tahlequah
1755 S Muskogee
74464
Phone (918) 456-8846
FAX (918) 456-3256
LVER: By Appointment
Counties Served:
Adair, Cherokee, and
Sequoyah

Tulsa
Counties Served:
Tulsa, Osage and
Pawnee
Tulsa Eastgate Center
14002 E. 21st St, Suite
1030 Phone (918) 796-
1200 FAX (918) 796-
1313
LVER: Kenneth
Harbuck
DVOP: Kelli Campbell
DVOP: OPEN apply
http://www.ok.gov/oesc
_web/

**Skyline Workforce
Center**
6128 E. 38th St, Suite
405, 74135
Phone (918) 384-2300
FAX (918) 384-2310
LVER: Brent Wheeler

*Woodward
1117 11th St 73801
Phone (580) 256-3308

Veterans Services
Chief, Veterans Services –
Paul Stephens
Phone (405) 557-7194

**Intensive Services
Coordinator**
James Taylor Phone
(405) 557-7281

http://veteranscrisisline.net/
http://www.militaryonesource.
mil/

Executive Secretary – Laurie
McCaffrey
Phone (405) 557-7193

Helpful Websites
www.OKMilitaryConnection.c
om
http://www.ok.gov/oesc_web
https://www.okjobmatch.com
http://www.onetonline.org
http://www.dol.gov/vets/
http://www.careeronestop.org
/
http://www.mynextmove.org/
vets/
http://www.va.gov/

General Resource Directory

Resource Referral

Referral Line Call 2-1-1 free 24-hour telephone number that connects people with important community services seven days a week, 365 days a year.

Clothing

CATHOLIC CHARITIES -
Clothing
2450 N Harvard, Tulsa
74158
918-949-4673
Serves: Tulsa County
T, W, Th, F 9 AM - 2 PM; T
4:30 PM - 6:30 PM; 3rd Sa
of each month 9 AM - 11
AM
Families can receive
assistance four times per
year; pregnant women can
receive monthly
assistance. Walk-in, no
appointment required.
Must be interviewed by a
caseworker.

Must provide one of the
following: photo
identification card, birth
certificate, insurance card,
passport or Social Security
card for household. Must
meet income guidelines.

CATHOLIC CHARITIES –
Coats for Kids
2450 N Harvard, Tulsa
74158
918-949-4673

Serves: Tulsa County
T, W, Th, F 10 AM - 2 PM
Seasonally (Nov. - Jan.)
provides Coats for Kids
offering coats to children or
adults in need. Must
provide identification for
household. Coat donation
drop-off at Tulsa area Yale
Cleaners.

CHRIST FOR HUMANITY
6314 E 13th St, Tulsa
74112
918-836-2424
Serves: Tulsa
M, T, W, Th 10 AM - 3 PM
Appointment required,
application form required.
Must provide photo
identification card(s).

DRESS FOR SUCCESS
1109 S Peoria, Tulsa
74120
918-599-8892
Serves: Tulsa County
M, T, W, Th, F 10 AM - 3
PM
Provides business
appropriate clothing to
women who are job
searching. Clients may
receive additional clothing
upon securing
employment.

Must have an appointment and professional referral.

FIRST BAPTIST
CHURCH OF TULSA
305 S Detroit, Tulsa 74120
918-587-6000
Serves: Tulsa County
M, T, W, Th 10 AM - 12 Noon
Walk-in; no appointment required.Must provide photo identification card(s), Social Security card, or birth certificates for household.
Must meet income guidelines.
GRACE CHURCH
9610 S Garnett Rd, Broken Arrow 74012 918-362-5265
March 2013
Serves: Tulsa County
Appointment Line: Th 9 AM - 12 Noon; Clothing Distributed: Sa 9 AM
Offers three items of clothing and one accessory per visit. Assistance limited to once per 30 day period. Appointment required. Must contact the appointment line to schedule an appointment. Must provide photo identification card(s) and proof of residence.

GUTS CHURCH
9120 E Broken Arrow Expwy, Tulsa 74145
918-622-3927
Serves: Tulsa County
F 10 AM - 12 noon walk-in; no appointment required.

JOHN 3:16 MISSION
2027 N Cincinnati, Tulsa 74106
918-592-1186
Serves: Tulsa County
Call to schedule an appointment: M, T, W, Th, F
9 AM - 5 PM.
Appointment times available: M, 2 PM and 5:30 PM; T, Th, F 11 AM - 2 PM; W 2
PM Assists persons in need with clothing; must attend chapel.
Appointment required.
Must provide photo identification card(s) and Social Security card(s) for household.

JOHN 3:16 MISSION –
MEN'S CLOTHING
506 North Cheyenne, Tulsa 74103
918-587-1187
Serves: Tulsa County
M, T, W, Th, F, Sa
10 AM - 11:30 PM
Provides clothing for men. Must sign in when arriving.

MINISTRY CENTER
312 S 33rd W Ave, Tulsa 74127
918-585-5310
Serves: Tulsa County
M, T, W, Th 9 AM - 2 PM
Provides emergency assistance with clothing. Spiritual guidance available. Appointment required. Must provide photo identification card(s)

and Social Security card(s).

NEIGHBOR FOR NEIGHBOR
505 E 36th St N, Tulsa 74106
918-425-5578
Serves: Tulsa County
M, T, W, Th, 9 AM - 12 noon, 1 PM - 3 PM
Provides financial assistance with items necessary to begin a job, including clothing and shoes for work.
Family Assistance will see the first 50 people to sign in at 9 AM and the first 50 to sign in at 1 PM each day. Must attend 1 hour life skills class in order to receive services unless 65 or older or have proof of permanent disability.

PARK PLAZA CHURCH OF CHRIST
4930 S Sheridan, Tulsa 74145 918-627-3201
Serves: Tulsa County
W 1 PM - 3 PM
Provides clothing for children and adults four times a year with 30 days between visits.
Walk-in; no appointment required.
Must provide proof of residence and photo identification card(s).

RIVERVIEW BAPTIST CHURCH
13201 S Memorial, Bixby 74008

918-369-2055
Serves: Tulsa County
M 10 AM - 12 noon; T 9:30 AM - 11:30 AM, and by appointment. Call about service availability.

TULSA DREAM CENTER
200 W 46th St N, Tulsa 74126
918-430-9984
Serves: Tulsa County
M, W, F 10 AM - 2 PM; T, Th, Sa 9 AM - 11:45 AM
Services are limited to two times per month.
ALDERSGATE UNITED METHODIST CHURCH
Alders Gator Aid
3702 S 90th E Avenue, Tulsa 74145
918-627-4165
Serves: 74112, 74129, 74134, 74145, 74146
3rd Sa 2 PM - 4 P
Walk-in; no appointment required.

CHURCH AT BATTLE CREEK - SAFE HARBOR
3025 N Aspen Ave, Broken Arrow 74012
918-355-3699
Serves: Broken Arrow
T 9:30 AM - 11 AM
Walk-in; no appointment required.
Must provide photo identification card(s).

BROKEN ARROW ASSEMBLY OF God
223 E College St, Broken Arrow 74012
918-251-8591
Serves: Broken Arrow

M, T, W, Th 10 AM - 2 PM
Must provide Social
Security numbers for
household; must provide
proof of residency.

BROKEN ARROW
NEIGHBORS
322 W Broadway Ave,
Broken Arrow 74012
918-251-7781
Serves: Broken Arrow
M, T, W, Th 9 AM - 3:30
PM
Provides clothing
distribution year round.
Seasonal clothing also
available for children and
adults.
Application form required.
Must provide proof of
address, proof of income,
photo identification card(s),
and copy of birth certificate
for all children.

EASTLAND ASSEMBLY
OF God
12310 E 21st St, Tulsa
74129
918-437-2590
Serves: 74108, 74112,
74128, 74129, 74134,
74145, 74146
T 6 PM - 7:30 PM (Third
Tuesday of each month)
Information form required.
Must be updated every six
months.
Must provide Social
Security card(s) for
household, proof of
address (preferably a utility
bill), photo identification
card.

May receive clothing once
every 30 days.

**Serves Southern Tulsa
County**

BIXBY COMMUNITY
OUTREACH CENTER
4 E Dawes Ave, Bixby
74008
918-366-9226
Serves: Kiefer, Mounds,
Haskell, Bixby, Glenpool,
Jenks, Leonard, Liberty
T 9 AM - 7 PM; W, Th 9
AM - 4 PM
Must provide current proof
of income and residency;
Social Security cards for
household.

**Serves Western Tulsa
County**

HARVEST HOUSE
1439 E 71st St, Tulsa
74136
918-492-5511 Serves:
74105, 74132, 74135,
74136. 74137
W 11:15 - 3 PM Contact
agency M 6 PM - 9 PM,
leave message, and
agency will return call to
schedule appointment.
Must provide photo
identification card(s) and
Social Security card(s).
Must meet income
guidelines. Service limited
to every two months.

**SAND SPRINGS
COMMUNITY SERVICES**
114 W 4th St, Sand
Springs 74063

918-245-5183
Serves: Sand Springs (live in 74063 or attend Sand Springs schools) M, T, W, Th 9 AM - 3 PM walk-in; no appointment required.
Must provide proof of residency, proof of income, Social Security card(s) for household, photo identification card(s).

WESTERN NEIGHBORS
4235 S.W. Blvd, Tulsa 74107
918-445-8840
Serves: 74107, 74132, 74131, 74050 and 74157
M, T, W, Th 8 AM - 12 noon
Must provide photo identification card(s) and proof of residency.

Serves Northern Tulsa County
FIRST BAPTIST CHURCH - SPERRY
301 W Main, Sperry 74073
918-288-7711
Serves: Sperry
1st and 3rd T 9 AM - 12 noon
Walk-ins accepted; call about service availability.
MANNA HOUSE MINISTRIES
4921 E Admiral Pl, Tulsa 74115
918-836-5541
Serves: 74104, 74110, 74112, 74115

T 11 AM - 1 PM; W 10 AM - 1 PM
Offers clothing assistance.

MISSION OWASSO LITTLE ANGELS ASSISTANCE MINISTRY
708 N Main, Owasso 74055
918-516-6638
Serves: Owasso and Collinsville
M, T, W, Th 10 AM - 2 PM; F 3 PM - 7 PM
Offers faith-based short-term helping hand for children ages 2 and under who need basic essential items on an emergency basis. Provides counseling and prayer to parents and care providers of infants and children.
Walk-in; no appointment required.

NEW HEIGHTS CHURCH OF OWASSO
106 N Main St, Owasso 74055
918-274-1725
Serves: Owasso
W 6 PM - 7 PM
Walk-in; no appointment required.

Diapers

EMERGENCY INFANT SERVICES
222 S Houston Ave, Tulsa
918-582-2469
Serves: Tulsa County
M, T, W, F 9 AM - 12:30 PM
Provides diapers, children's and maternity clothes. Assistance available for children 5 and younger and pregnant women.
Walk-in; no appointment required.

Must provide photo identification card(s).
Acceptable forms of income, valid driver's (ID) for minor children are: birth certificate, hospital birth certificate with foot prints, WIC folder, immunization card or school records with birth date.
Must meet income guidelines.

EMERGENY INFANT SERVICES - EASTIDE
990 E 42nd St, Ste 100, Tulsa 918-582-2469
Serves: 74127, 74126, 74130, 74106, 74103, 74104, 74114, 74105, 74107, 74131, 74132, 74135, 74110, 74117, 74115, 74116 T, W, Th, F, Sa 9 AM - 12:30 PM

Provides diapers, children's and maternity clothes. Assistance available for children 5 and younger and pregnant women.
Walk-in; no appointment required.
Must provide photo identification card(s).
Acceptable forms of ID for minor children are: birth certificate, hospital birth certificate with foot prints, WIC folder, immunization card or school records with birth date.
Must meet income guidelines.

GLENPOOL OUTREACH CENTER COVERED BOTTOMS DIAPER BANK
596 W 141st St, Glenpool 74033
918-321-2302
Serves: Glenpool, Keifer, Mounds, Liberty Mounds
2nd & 3rd Tu 9:30 AM - 1:30 PM
Provides diapers up to size six and adult depends undergarments.
Walk-in; no appointment needed.
Must provide proof of residency and photo identification card(s).

HARVEST HOUSE
1439 E 71st St, Tulsa 74136

918-492-5511 Serves:
74105, 74132, 74135,
74136. 74137
W 11:15 AM - 3 PM
Offers clothing, diapers
and formula.
Contact agency M 6 PM - 9
PM to make an
appointment for
Wednesday.

Must provide photo
identification card(s),
Social Security card(s),
vouchers for WIC and/or
Food Stamps. Must be
mother with children 0 - 3
years of age, or up to the
4th birthday.

CRISIS LINES AND HOTLINES AIDS/HIV
Health Outreach Prevention Education (HOPE) HIV/
STD Hotline 800-535-2437 ⍰ National AIDS Hotline 800-232-4636

CRIME
Crime Stoppers
918-596-2677

DEAF & HARD OF HEARING
TSHA (Assistance for Deaf/Hard of Hearing)
918-832-8742

DISABILITY
Ability Resources Disability Information Line
918-592-1235

DOMESTIC VIOLENCE/ABUSE/RAPE
Call Rape 918-7HELPME (918-743-5763)
Oklahoma Safeline
(Domestic Violence, Sexual Assault,
Stalking)
800-522-7233

Child/Elder Abuse Hotline 800-522-3511

Domestic Violence Intervention Services (DVIS)
918-743-5763

GAMBLING
Problem Gambling Helpline 800-522-4700

INFORMATION & REFERRAL
211 Helpline Information & Referral 2-1-1

Child Care Resource Center Child Care Provider
Referral 918-834-2273

City of Tulsa Mayor's Action Center
918-596-2100

Library Research Center (ASKUS Hotline)
918-549-7323

Tele Ayuda Spanish-Language Information & Referral
918-663-0001

MENTAL HEALTH
COPES Mobile Mental Health Crisis Team 918-744-4800
MHAT Mental Health Assistance Center 918-382-2482
Reach Out Hotline (Mental Health/Substance Abuse
Crisis) 800-522-9054

CALM Center (adolescent crisis) 918-394-CALM
Center for Behavioral Health 918-293-2100

POISON CONTROL/FOOD ALLERGIES
Food Allergy and Anaphylaxis Network 800-929-4040
Oklahoma Poison Control Center 800-222-1222

PRENATAL Care
Babyline Prenatal Appointment Line 918-838-0694

SENIORS
INCOG AAA Senior Assistance Line 918-579-9486
SeniorLine 918-664-9000

SUICIDE PREVENTION
COPES Mobile Mental Health Crisis Team 918-744-4800
2-1-1 Heartline Suicide Prevention Hotline 405-848-2273
National Suicide Prevention LifeLine   800-273-8255
Trevor Project (Crisis/Suicide Prevention for
Gay/Lesbian/Transgender/Questioning Youth) 866-488-
7386

VETERANS

Iraq & Afghanistan Veterans of America	212-982-9699
Military One Source	800-342-9647
National Military Family Association	800-260-0218
National Veterans Suicide Prevention Hotline	800-273-8255
United Service Organization (USO)	703-908-6400
Wounded Soldier and Family Hotline	800-984-8523

YOUTH

National Runaway Hotline	800-786-2929
Youth Services Crisis Line	918-582-0061

Emergency Shelter

DAY CENTER FOR THE HOMELESS - Homeless
Individuals and Families
415 W Archer, Tulsa 74103
918-583-5588 Serves: Tulsa County
Su, M, T, W, Th, F, Sa 5:30 PM -7 AM
Offers night shelter with dinner and light breakfast; showers, towels
and toiletry items, sleeping mat, sheet and blanket provided.
Must provide TB card at front desk (grace period allowed for new
guests).
Must be a homeless individual or family.

DAYSPRING VILLA - Domestic Violence
Confidential Location, Sand Springs
918-245-4075 Serves: Tulsa County
Su, M, T, W, Th, F, Sa 24 hours

Provides a safe, confidentially located, faith-based domestic violence
shelter for up to 55 women and children in crisis. Contact agency for
initial telephone intake. Must be a female, age 18 years of age or
older, in need of emergency shelter and willing to follow house rules.
Children except teen-age boys are allowed to stay with their mother.
Pregnant women are accepted.

DAYSPRING VILLA - PROJECT DARK2LIGHT -
Survivors of Human Trafficking
Confidential Location, Sand Springs
918-245-4075 Serves: Tulsa County
Su, M, T, W, Th, F, Sa 24 hours provides emergency shelter, medical
services, food, clothing, and spiritual guidance with helping Survivors
of sexual human trafficking set practical goals to discover

independence and self-sufficiency. Contact agency for initial telephone intake. Must be a Survivor of sexual human trafficking. Must be female to stay in shelter. Males will be referred to other resources.

DOMESTIC VIOLENCE INTERVENTION
SERVICES/CALL RAPE - Domestic Violence
Confidential Location, Tulsa
918-743-5763 Serves: Tulsa County
Su, M, T, W, Th, F, Sa 24 hours provides temporary lodging and meals, counseling and supportive services for Survivors of domestic violence, dating violence, sexual assault, sexual trafficking, and stalking and their children. Counseling and case management for adults and children is available on-site as well as child care.

JOHN 3:16 MISSION - Homeless Men
506 N Cheyenne, Tulsa 74103
918-587-1187 Serves: Tulsa County
April 2013 provides homeless services.
Must provide income information.
Shelter is restricted to men only; other services are available to families.

SALVATION ARMY - CENTER OF HOPE -
Homeless Individuals and Families
102 N Denver Ave, Tulsa 74103
918-582-7201 Serves: Tulsa County
Su, M, T, W, Th, F, Sa, 24 hours provides emergency shelter for homeless individuals, families or those in need of temporary housing. Residents receive morning and evening meals. (Pregnant women are accepted).
Check in at 4:30 PM daily; provide written proof of TB test within 72 hours of admittance. Interview with case manager.

SURAYYA ANNE FOUNDATION - Women &
Children 8508 S 71st E Ave, Tulsa 74133
918-282-2362 Serves: Tulsa
Provides long-term or short-term housing for women and children who are disadvantaged, sick, homeless, or abused with a focus on reintegrating back into society. Off-site services are offered for those who qualify. Application form required, appointment preferred. Must provide photo identification card(s), list of services currently receiving, eviction notice, cut of notice.

TULSA COUNTY SOCIAL SERVICES -
Homeless Individuals and Families

2401 Charles Page Blvd, Tulsa 74127
918-596-5591 Serves: Tulsa County
Su, M, T, W, Th, F, Sa 24 hours provides emergency/temporary housing, food, medical care, clothing. Focused on families and children. Pregnant women are accepted. All residents must submit to TB screening as a condition of service. Life Skill and Parenting Classes are also available.
Interview required. Must provide photo identification card(s) and proof of income.
Must intend to reside in Tulsa County. Must be ambulatory and able to care for own physical needs.

YOUTH SERVICES OF TULSA - Youth
1011 E 4th St, Tulsa 74120
918-382-4450 Serves: Tulsa County
Su, M, T, W, Th, F, Sa 24 hours provides an adolescent emergency shelter providing temporary residence for runaways, homeless youths, youths experiencing serious conflict with their family and youths awaiting placement or returning from placement in public or private institutions. Must be ages 12 - 18 with parental or legal consent.

Housing
Low-Income Apartments:

The Yacht Club
Apartments (more info)
Neighborhood: Midtown
studio to two bedroom
apartments from $385 to
$620
Call: (866) 710-9791

Lakewood Gardens
Apartments (more info)
Tulsa, OK 74135
Neighborhood: Midtown
1 to 2 bedroom apartments
from $490 to $595
Call: (866) 767-8385

Pepper Tree Apartments
Tulsa, OK 74136
1 to 2 bedroom apartments
from $625 to $779

Call: (918) 925-9626

The Enclave at Brookside
1 to 2 bedroom apartments
from $950 to $1980
Call: (918) 770-0191

Reserve at Elm
Apartments
Reserve at Elm
Apartments (more info)
Jenks, OK 74037
studio to two bedroom
apartments from $780 to
$1080
Call: (918) 615-2036

St. Thomas Square
Apartments
Tulsa, OK 74136

1 to 2 bedroom
apartments: Call for rates
Call: (877) 356-2197

Villas at Yorktown
Tulsa, OK 74105 studio to
two bedroom apartments
from $340 to $640
Call: (918) 379-1017

Prescott Woods
Apartments
Tulsa, OK 74136
Neighborhood: South
Tulsa
studio to two bedroom
apartments from $399 to
$569
Call: (877) 713-6519

Observation Pointe
Apartments
Tulsa, OK 74134 1 to 2
bedroom apartments from
$399 to $599 Call: (866)
446-5371

Coppermill Apartments
1 to 2 bedroom apartments
from $409 to $569
Call: (855) 415-3077

Tulsa Housing Authority-
Public Housing
Apache Manor
2402 North Marion
Tulsa, OK 74115 (918)
834-4236

Comanche Park
3608 North Quaker
Tulsa, OK 74106
(918) 425-7539

East Central Village
12330 East Archer

Tulsa, OK 74116
(918) 438-4020

Hewgley Terrace
420 South Lawton
(918) 584-0063

LaFortune Tower
1725 Southwest Boulevard
Tulsa, OK 74107
(918) 583-0784

Mohawk Manor
3637 North Birmingham
Tulsa, OK 74110
(918) 425-0022

Parkview Terrace
1615 West 59th Street
Tulsa, OK 74107
(918) 446-6154

Pioneer Plaza
901 North Elgin
Tulsa, OK 74106
(918) 584-2554

Riverview Park
2212 South Jackson
Tulsa, OK 74107
(918) 583-7506

Sandy Park
6301 West 11th Place
Tulsa, OK 74127
(918) 245-5981

Seminole Hills
1624 East Virgin
Tulsa, OK 74107
(918) 583-1581
South Haven Manor
4012 West 56th Place
Tulsa, OK 74107
(918) 446-2530

Homeless Drop In Centers
DAY CENTER FOR THE HOMELESS
415 W Archer, Tulsa 74103
918-583-5588 Serves: Tulsa County
Su, M, T, W, Th, F, Sa 8 AM - 4 PM
Provides a safe place to rest, food, restrooms and bathing facilities, personal care items, laundry facilities and a change of clothing. Clients may also make and receive phone calls, receive mail and store personal items in an open storage area. Other programs and services are available on-site from Veterans Administration, Social Security Administration, Oklahoma Department of Human Services, and 12 &12 Substance Abuse Outreach. On-site services provided by DHS, VA, SS, Mental Health Outreach, Family and Children's Services and HOPE HIV/AIDS testing. There are also Nurse Triage Clinic and Community Voice Mail services.

Must provide TB card (grace period allowed for new guests). Any homeless person; homeless children must be accompanied by an adult.

JOHN 3:16 WOMEN'S DAY PROGRAM
506 N Cheyenne, Tulsa 74103
918-587-1187
Serves: Tulsa County
M, T, W, Th, F 9 AM - 3 PM
Offers faith-based support services and day room for women. Services include case management, pastoral counseling, Bible study, prayer, presentation of the Gospel, educational classes, peer support and group discussion for relapse prevention and trauma recovery. Walk-in; no appointment required.
Must be homeless woman without children.

MENTAL HEALTH ASSOCIATION IN TULSA -
DENVER HOUSE
1729 S Denver Ave, Tulsa 74119
918-382-2435
Serves: Creek County, Okmulgee County, Osage County, Rogers County, Tulsa County, Wagoner County
T, W, Th 11 AM - 7 PM; F, Sa 12 Noon - 9 PM
Provides a non-clinical, non-coercive, supportive environment for adults experiencing the challenges of a mental illness, or co-occurring disorder to learn different methods of living.
Must be 18 years of age or older.
Must have mental illness or co-occurring disorder.

YOUTH SERVICES OF TULSA
311 S Madison, Tulsa 74120
918-582-0061
Serves: Tulsa County
T, W, Th 12 PM - 5 PM
Builds trust with homeless youth by meeting basic needs through
Outreach and Drop In Center. Links homeless youth with community
services.
Must be ages 16 - 24.

Home Improvement/Accessibility
NEIGHBOR FOR NEIGHBOR
505 E 36th St N, Tulsa 74106
918-425-5578 Serves: Tulsa County
Assists low-income families in becoming home owners by using a
type of "work equity" as a down payment. Homes that require all
levels of renovation are purchased by or donated to NFN and used for
this program. This program also repairs and renovates homes.
Application form required. Must complete a prerequisite application
process and a minimum of 150 hours of work in the housing program.

REBUILDING TOGETHER TULSA
701 S Main, Tulsa 74119 918-742-6241
Serves: City of Tulsa Offers modest home repairs to homes owned by
low-income elderly and/or disabled Tulsans, using volunteer labor and
donated materials. Repairs may include: roof repair, energy efficiency,
wheelchair ramps, exterior handrails, carpentry, minor electrical,
minor plumbing, exterior paint, etc.
Application required. Must provide proof of income for the household,
proof of ownership, copy of current property tax bill. Must be low-
income homeowner, who is over 60 or living with a disability. Must
own home in Tulsa County and live in the home at time of application.

WORKING IN NEIGHBORHOODS
175 E 2nd St 5th Fl, Tulsa 74120
918-576-5552 Serves: City of Tulsa
M, T, W, Th, F 8 AM - 5 PM Grants up to $5,000 to repair basic
components of homes owned and occupied by low-income
individuals.
Includes the Emergency Repair Program and the Rehab Loan
Program. Basic components include: electrical system, plumbing,
structural components, security, heating, gas lines, or any component
that would pose an immediate threat to the health and safety of

occupants if not repaired. Must provide proof of home ownership, proof of employment and proof of income.

Home Purchase/Housing Counseling/Foreclosure Assistance

COMMUNITY ACTION PROJECT OF TULSA COUNTY
4606 S Garnett Rd Ste 100, Tulsa 74146
918-382-3247
Serves: City of Tulsa
Offers pre- and post-purchase housing counseling, down payment assistance, and predatory lending education.
Contact agency for class times. Appointment required. Registration for class required.

CREDIT COUNSELING CENTER - BROKEN ARROW
317 S Main, Broken Arrow 74012
918-259-0164
Serves: Tulsa County
M, T, W, Th, F 8 AM - 5 PM; Evenings and Sa by appointment.
Provides comprehensive housing counseling for individuals interested in owning their own home or behind in rent or mortgage payments.
Contact agency to meet with a certified counselor in-person or talk over the phone.

CREDIT COUNSELING CENTERS OF OKLAHOMA
4646 S Harvard, Tulsa 74135
918-744-5611
Serves: Tulsa County
M, T, W, Th, F 8 AM - 5 PM; Sa 8:30 AM - 12 noon; Evenings by appointment.
Provides comprehensive housing counseling for individuals interested in owning their own home, behind in rent or mortgage payments or wanting to know about a reverse mortgage. ·
Contact agency to meet with a certified counselor in person or talk over the phone, or submit information over the website.

DEBT REDUCTION SERVICES
4111 Darlington Ave, Tulsa 74135
918-660-0200
Serves: Tulsa County
M, T, W, Th, F 9 AM - 6 PM, Sa 9 AM - 1 PM
Provides assistance in preparing a credit report review, budgeting, webinars/seminars, and debt management.

Appointment required.
Must provide monthly bill statements, credit card statements, photo ID, income verification, and additional documentation may be requested.

HOMEOWNER'S HOPE HOTLINE
3033 Excelsior Blvd, Minneapolis, MN 55416
888-995-4673
Serves: Oklahoma
Su, M, T, W, Th, F, Sa 24 hours
Offers foreclosure assistance and housing counseling services.

LEGAL AID SERVICES OF OKLAHOMA
907 S Detroit, Tulsa 74120
888-534-5243
Serves: Tulsa County
M, T, W, Th, F 8:30 AM - 5 PM
Provides assistance with application for a loan modification under the Home Affordable Modification Program, negotiation with the mortgage servicer regarding payments not credited, insurance or tax escrow issues, reinstatement, etc., representation in Court to contest the foreclosure and Chapter 13 bankruptcy to stop the foreclosure.

Make A' Move Housing
3702 S Elm Pl #502
Broken Arrow, OK 74011
Online-Certified 1st Time Homebuyer Education
www.makeamovehusing.org
*Upto $7000 in closing cost assistance

METROPOLITAN TULSA URBAN LEAGUE
240 E Apache St, Tulsa 74106
918-584-0001
Serves: Counseling and Education: Tulsa County
Down Payment Assistance: City of Tulsa
M, T, W, Th, F 8 AM - 5 PM;
Home buyer education: 3rd Sa of the month, 9 AM - 3 PM
Provides home buyer education, counseling and down payment assistance. Provides foreclosure prevention counseling and fair housing counseling and education.
Contact agency to enroll.
Counseling and Education Services: No restrictions
Down Payment Assistance: Must meet financial eligibility requirements.

US DEPT OF HOUSING AND URBAN DEVELOPMENT
2 W Second St Ste 400, Tulsa 74103
800-569-4287 Serves: Tulsa County
M, T, W, Th, F 8 AM - 4:30 PM
Offers a national call center for assistance on FHA (Federal Housing
Administration) lending. Assists with preventing foreclosures and loan
extensions.
Receives reports of discriminatory housing practices.

Landlord/Tenant Assistance

EARLY SETTLEMENT MEDIATION - TULSA OFFICE
600 Civic Center, Tulsa 74103
918-596-7786
Serves: Tulsa County
M, T, W, Th, F 8 AM - 12 noon, 1 PM - 5 PM
Offers Landlord/Tenant dispute assistance to include: maintenance
problems, deposits and termination of tenancy.

LEGAL AID SERVICES OF OKLAHOMA - TULSA

907 S Detroit, Tulsa 74120
888-534-5243
Serves: Tulsa County
M, T, W, Th, F 8:30 AM - 5 PM
Provides assistance with civil legal problems such as foreclosure and
eviction.
Application available online
Must meet Federal income guidelines.
Homeless Financial Assistance Programs

SUPPORTIVE SERVICES FOR VETERAN FAMILIES

Community Service Council
111 W 5th St, Tulsa 74103   Dial 2-1-1 Serves: Tulsa County
Must contact 2-1-1 Helpline Su, M, T, W, Th, F, Sa 24 hours. SSVF
provides supportive services to very low-income Veterans and their
families residing in or transitioning to permanent housing. Provides
financial assistance and case management services for households
at-risk of becoming homeless and re-housing assistance for

Homeless Veterans and their families. Must call 2-1-1 to complete pre-screen survey with 2-1-1 call specialist for referral to program. Do not call main drug Court number for SSVF. All SSVF referrals must first come through 2-1-1 Helpline pre-screen survey. Must provide discharge paperwork.
Must meet residency, income, housing and discharge criteria on 2-1-1 pre-screen.

Housing Search and Information
LIFE SENIOR SERVICES
5950 E 31st St, Tulsa 74135
918-664-9000 Serves: Oklahoma
M, T, W, Th, F 8 AM - 5 PM Publishes the Vintage Guide to Housing and Services, a comprehensive guide to senior resources. Available at Life Senior Services and online at www.seniorline.org.

MENTAL HEALTH ASSOCIATION IN TULSA
3322 E 30th St, Tulsa 74114 918-382-2475
Serves: Tulsa
M, T, W, Th, F 8 AM - 5 PM
Offers affordable housing options to include all-billspaid apartments located in Tulsa.

TULSAHOUSINGSEARCH.ORG
PO Box 35305, Charlotte, NC 28235
Serves: Tulsa County
Offers information about market rate and subsidized housing options.
Website: www.tulsahousingsearch.org.

Low-Income/Subsidized Rental Housing
HOUSING AUTHORITY - TULSA 415 E Independence, Tulsa 74106
www.tulsahousing.org
Serves: Tulsa Provides public housing for qualified low-income families, Veterans, the elderly and disabled.
The Housing Choice Voucher Program is responsible for families receiving rental assistance where they can select housing of their choice, whether it is an apartment, duplex or house, provided the owner of the unit is willing to accept the family under the Voucher Program guidelines.
Online application form required. Must meet income guidelines.

Rent Payment Assistance

AMERICAN LEGION OF TULSA
11328 E Admiral Pl, Tulsa 74116
918-437-4308 Serves: Tulsa
AIDS in obtaining financial aid from Oklahoma Department of
Veterans Affairs for shelter and utilities. Applicants must be honorably
discharged Veterans or their families who served a minimum of 90
days during a war or national emergency and who have resided in
Oklahoma for more than one year. Financial assistance given only in
case of true emergency such as death, disaster, sickness or accident.
Unemployment is not a basis for payment. Must provide a certified
copy of DD214 or discharge papers showing dates of service.
Interview will determine need for other documents.

BIXBY OUTREACH CENTER
4 E Dawes Ave, Bixby 74008
918-366-9226
Serves: Bixby
T, W, Th 9 AM - 4 PM ⬜   Offers rent assistance.
Must have current proof of income, current proof of address, Social
Security cards for all household members.

BROKEN ARROW NEIGHBORS
322 W Broadway Ave, Broken Arrow 74012
918-251-7781
Serves: Broken Arrow
M, T, W, Th 9 AM - 4 PM
Provides rent assistance.
Walk-in; no appointment required.
Must provide current proof of address, proof of ID license or photo
identification card, and copy of birth certificate for all children, for all
services. Must provide copy of eviction notice.

CATHOLIC CHARITIES
2450 N Harvard, Tulsa 74158
918-949-4673 Serves: Tulsa County
F 9 AM until capacity is reached
Provides limited amounts of financial assistance for rent. Will only
assist with up to the last $100.00 after the remaining balance has
been pledged or paid. Clients must appear in person. Assistance is
given on a first come first serve basis.
Must provide a copy of lease agreement.

HELPING HANDS MINISTRY

712 S Boston, Tulsa 74119
918-582-1356
Serves: Tulsa County
M, T, W, Th, F 9 AM - 12 noon, or until funds depleted.
Offers payment based on eviction notice amount. Clients are helped once in 12 months on an emergency basis. No deposit fees available.
Walk-in; no appointment required.
Must provide photo identification card(s), Social Security card(s), and landlord eviction notice.

RESTORE HOPE MINISTRIES
2960 Charles Page Blvd, Tulsa 74127
918-878-7999
Serves: Tulsa County
M, T, W 9 AM - 12 noon; Th 9 AM - 11 AM
Provides rent assistance. Call rent hotline for phone screening. At present time, program does not assist with clients who are currently receiving other housing assistance (Section 8/THA/HUD).
Appointment required.

SAND SPRINGS COMMUNITY SERVICES
4th & Garfield, Sand Springs 74063
918-245-5183
Serves: Sand Springs
M, T, W, Th 9AM - 3PM
Provides assistance with up to $200 in rent payments. Client must first arrange for the amount over $200 to be paid. Client may receive assistance once per year.
Walk-in; no appointment required.
Must provide photo identification card, proof of residency, proof of income, Social Security card for each member of household, and eviction notice.
Sand Springs residents only - must live within 74063 zip code or attend Sand Springs schools.

Utility Assistance
AMERICAN LEGION CARSON WILSON RIGNEY
FORRESTER SHOEMAKER POST 1
1120 E 8th St, Tulsa 74120
918-584-4274 Serves: Tulsa
T, Th 9 AM - 2 PM, M, F 9 AM - 12 PM
Offers utility assistance in case of true emergency such as death, disaster, sickness or accident. Unemployment is not a basis for payment.

Must be a veteran or have a veteran living in the home. Must provide a certified copy of DD214 or discharge papers showing dates of service. Interview will determine need for other documents.

BIXBY OUTREACH CENTER
4 E Dawes Ave, Bixby 74008
918-366-9226 Serves: Bixby
T, W, Th 9 AM - 4 PM Offers assistance with utilities. Must be a Bixby resident. Must have cut-off notice.

BROKEN ARROW NEIGHBORS
322 W Broadway Ave, Broken Arrow 74012
918-251-7781 Serves: Broken Arrow
M, T, W, Th 9 AM - 4 PM provides utility assistance. Walk-in; no appointment required.
Clients are required to have current proof of address, proof of income, valid driver's license or (ID), and copy of birth certificate for all children, for all services. Must provide utility service cut-off notice. Must live in Broken Arrow.

CATHOLIC CHARITIES
2450 N Harvard, Tulsa 74158
918-949-4673 Serves: Tulsa County
F 9 AM until capacity is reached
Clients must appear in person. Assistance is given on a first come first serve basis. Must provide valid identification, such as a drivers license, birth certificate, passport, etc. Must provide a copy of the utility bill with the cut-off notice.

FIRST BAPTIST CHURCH OF TULSA
305 S Detroit, Tulsa 74120
918-587-6068
Serves: Tulsa County
M 8:30 AM - 9:30 AM
Provides help with utility bill payments. Assists 20 per week. Appointment required. Must meet income guidelines.

HARVEST HOUSE
1439 E 71st St, Tulsa 74136
918-492-5511
Serves: 74105, 74132, 74135, 74136, 74137
Contact agency M 6 PM - 9 PM, leave message, and agency will contact to schedule appointment.
Provides utility assistance for cut-off notice; $25.00 limit. Clients are limited to utility assistance no more than every 4 months as funds are available.

Must provide photo identification card(s), Social Security card(s), and a copy of bill with cut-off notice.
Must have cut-off notice.

HELPING HANDS MINISTRY
712 S Boston, Tulsa 74119
918-582-1356
Serves: Tulsa County
M, T, W, Th, F 9 AM - 12 noon, or until funds depleted.
Offers limited utility assistance when funds available. Clients are helped once in 12 months on an emergency basis. No help is available for TANF clients who live in subsidized housing. No utility deposits are available.
Walk-in; no appointment required.
Must provide photo identification card(s), Social Security card(s), and cut-off notice.

NEIGHBOR FOR NEIGHBOR
505 E 36th St N, Tulsa 74106
918-425-5578
Serves: Tulsa County
M, T, W, Th 9 AM - 12 noon, 1 PM - 3 PM
Offers small loans if client has cut-off notice; funds are depleted early.
Must provide cut-off notice, photo ID, and Social Security card(s).

NEIGHBORS ALONG THE LINE
5000 W Charles Page Blvd, Tulsa 74127
918-582-3491 Serves: 74127 within boundaries (East bound, Hwy 244, North boundary Edison St., South boundary, Arkansas River; West boundary, 81st W. Ave)
By appointment only. Offers utility assistance.
Must provide proof of residency, proof of income, photo identification card(s), and Social Security cards for the household and copy of current utility cut-off notice.

OWASSO COMMUNITY RESOURCES
109 N Birch, Owasso 74055
918-272-4969 Serves: Collinsville, Owasso
M, T, W 9 AM - 2 PM; Th 1 PM - 6 PM
Provides financial assistance on an emergency basis to prevent cut-off of gas, water or electric utilities. Application form required.
Must provide photo ID; Social Security card for every household member including children; Proof of Owasso or Collinsville Residency (rent/mortgage contract, current utility bill); most recent statement of income (pay stub, SSI, unemployment, disability, worker's comp, food stamps, welfare, etc.).

Limited to once every 12 months. All other financial resources must be exhausted. Must be within 5 days of cut-off. Late fees and deposits are ineligible.

SALVATION ARMY - TULSA LOCATION
102 N Denver Ave, Tulsa 74103
918-582-7201
Serves: Tulsa County
By appointment. Call for appointment M, T, W, Th 2 PM - 2:30 PM
Provides emergency financial assistance for utility bills and deposits. Help may be received once in a 12 ⬚ month period.
Must have utility bill, ID, proof of income, and other documentation may be required.

SAND SPRINGS COMMUNITY SERVICES
4th & Garfield, Sand Springs 74063
918-245-5183
Serves: Sand Springs
M, T, W, Th 9 AM - 3 PM
Provides assistance with up to $150 for gas or electric payments and up to $50 for water payments. Client must first pay amount over $150/$50. Client may receive assistance once per year.
Walk-in; no appointment required.
Must provide photo identification card(s), proof of residency, proof of income, Social Security card for household, and have cut-off notice. Sand Springs residents only - must live within 74063 zip code or have City of Sand Springs water service.

WESTERN NEIGHBORS
4235 Southwest Blvd, Tulsa 74107
918-445-8840
Serves: Tulsa south and west of the Arkansas River, south to Jenks city limits, west to Prattville. Serves zip codes 74107, 74132, 74131, 74050 and 74157.
Provides utility assistance payments (when funds are available) for past-due/cut-off utilities.
Appointment required.
Must provide identification and proof of residency. Must be a resident of Southwest Tulsa with a stated need.

Spotlight Dental & Healthcare
Discount Dental & Health Plans
www.discountdentalhealthplans.org
$19.95 (Household)
30 DAY MONEY BACK GUARANTEE

- No Paperwork
- No Waiting
- Choose from almost 75,000 dental providers in the AmeriPlan network
- 25% to 80% savings on dental procedures performed by a Program dentist
- Special savings on specialist work such as braces, oral surgery, root canals, gum treatment and children's dentistry

Grassroots Healthcare

Hours:
Monday - Friday
8:30 - 5:00
Closed 11:30 - 12:30 for lunch
Closed Saturday & Sunday

Location:
6530 E. 91st St.
Tulsa, OK 74133
(918) 878-7733
Fax (918) 878-7736.

Dr. Metilda Tate M.D.
High-quality medical care for an affordable price.
By eliminating insurance they offer everything for your general medical needs.

Pricing:
$20 New Patient Fee

Level I Simple $49
(Complaint specific, examples: strep throat, cough, poison ivy) does not include tests such as lab/x-ray or procedures

Level II Complex $59-$69
(Examples HTN, DMII, stable chronic illness)

Level III Complicated $79-$89

(Medical management with or without exacerbation, CAD, ADD, ADHD, COPD, Respiratory)

Well-Child Check
+$20 for child's first visit
<1 yr.........$50
1-4 yr.........$60
5-11 yr.......$65
12-17 yr.....$70

Full Physical Includes lab: urine, blood count, liver, electrolytes, kidney functions, thyroid, cholesterol, prostate (men), PAP (women)
(no EKG) $125 (with EKG) $155
Sports Physical....$25

Procedures:
Simple Laceration (all materials included) <2cm $125
Boil Drainage (includes repeat packing) $125
Ear flush (per ear) $15
Skin Lesion Removal $125+office visit
Joint Injection/Aspiration $125+office visit
Trigger Point Injection $25 - 1st, $10 each additional office visit

Lab Fees $20 with an office visit
(Plus the cost of the lab procedure listed below, physician interpretation is included)
We offer steeply discounted labs.
Wellness Panel (fasting) (CBC, CMP, TSH, cholesterol panel) $65

Blood count	$20
Kidney and electrolytes	$15
Liver, kidney and electrolytes	$20
Thyroid	$15
Urine	$10
HgA1C	$20
Strep	$15
Mono	$20
Flu	$20
RSV	$20
Prostate	$20
Pap	$50
Lipid panel	$20
Liver panel	$25
Statin panel (liver & lipids)	$35
PT/INR	$15
Throat culture	Wet prep
Urine culture	Uric acid
Wound culture	Sexually transmitted disease panel

Hepatitis panel	$25
HIV	$20
Vit D	$70
Vit B12	$70
Testosterone level	$30
sed rate	$65
C-reactive protein	$25
Rheumatology panel	$65
	$20
$20	$20
$20	$65
$40	

Other Lab services are available. Please visit our office for a complete list and pricing.
We do not endorse or represent Grassroots, the information above is only for informational purposes. The information listed above was taken directly from website: http://www.grassrootstulsa.com/index.html

United Way Partner Agencies

12 & 12, Inc.
918-664-4224 www.12and12.org
Provides a full range of drug and alcohol treatment programs focused on a person's specific needs, regardless of their ability to pay.

A New Leaf
918-451-1491 www.anewleaf.org
Supports children and adults with developmental disabilities via residential respite, living skills classes, vocational training/placement.

Ability Resources
918-592-1235 www.ability-resources.org
Provides services and information to help people with disabilities attain and maintain personal independence.

American Red Cross, Tulsa Area Chapter
918-831-1100 http://www.redcross.org/ok/tulsa
Helps families prevent, prepare for and respond to emergencies, and provides community health education and training programs.

Big Brothers Big Sisters of Oklahoma
918-744-4400 www.bbbsok.org

Facilitates one-to-one mentoring friendships between children and caring volunteers through community-based and site-based programs.

Boy Scouts of America, Indian Nations Council
918-743-6125 www.okscouts.org
A year round program providing character building programs focused on leadership, life skills and outdoor learning for youth 7 to 21.

The Bridges Foundation
918-592-3333 www.thebridgesfound.org
Provides employment services and living skills training for adults with developmental disabilities.

Bristow Social Services, Inc.
918-367-5400 www.bristowhelps.org
Provides help for those in crisis with emergency utility assistance, prescription assistance, clothing and more.

Broken Arrow Neighbors
918-251-7781 www.baneighbors.com
Provides basic needs assistance to financially disadvantaged residents of Broken Arrow.

Broken Arrow Seniors
918-259-8377 www.baseniors.org
Provides programs and services that help seniors maintain a healthy, independent lifestyle.

Camp Fire Green Country Council
918-592-2267 www.tulsacampfire.org
Provides asset-building programs and activities for boys and girls,

Pre-K through 12th grade, and their families.
Caring Community Friends
918-224-6464 www.caringcommunityfriends.org
Provides prescriptions, medical supplies, food, clothing, and utility assistance for families and individuals.

Center for Employment Opportunities
918-894-6561 www.ceoworks.org

Dedicated to providing immediate, effective and comprehensive employment services to men and women with recent criminal convictions.

The Center for Individuals with Physical Challenges
918-584-8607 www.tulsacenter.org
Provides a variety of rehabilitative fitness, adaptive recreation and community outings for people with physical challenges.

Child Abuse Network
918-624-0200 www.childabusenetwork.org
Brings multiple agencies together under one roof to provide non-traumatic child abuse investigation and crisis intervention services.

Circle of Care - Frances E. Willard Ministry Center
918-583-9506 www.circleofcare.org
Provides services to support foster care families, along with transitional housing and services for homeless women and their children.

Community Action Project of Tulsa County
918-382-3200 www.captc.org
Helps individuals and families in economic need achieve self-sufficiency through early childhood education and asset-building services.

Community Service Council of Greater Tulsa
918-585-5551 www.csctulsa.org
Provides leadership for community-based planning and action to prevent and reduce social and health problems.

Credit Counseling Centers of Oklahoma
918-744-5611 www.cccsofok.org
Provides money management and credit education through confidential counseling sessions and community workshops.

Creek County Literacy Program
918-224-9647 www.creekliteracy.org
Provides free confidential tutoring for adults and children.

Crossroads, Inc.
918-749-2141 www.crossroadsok.org

A psychosocial clubhouse model program that provides hope, opportunities and choices for adults who have a mental illness.

Crosstown Learning Center
918-582-1457 www.crosstowntulsa.org
Provides early educational opportunities in a nurturing environment for children and families.

Domestic Violence Intervention Services (DVIS)/Call Rape
918-743-5763 www.dvis.org
Provides counseling, shelter, transitional living, Court advocacy and education services to families affected by domestic and sexual violence.

Eastern Oklahoma Donated Dental Services
918-742-5544 www.eodds.org
Free dental care for low-income seniors and individuals with disabilities in eastern Oklahoma (918 area code region).

Family & Children's Services
918-587-9471 www.fcsok.org
Provides behavioral health care, child abuse, early childhood family support and family life education services across the lifespan.

Girl Scouts of Eastern Oklahoma
918-749-2551 www.gseok.org
A leadership development experience for girls 5-17 who discover, connect and take action to make the world a better place.

Goodwill Industries of Tulsa
918-584-7291 www.goodwilltulsa.org
Provides work opportunities, job training and support services for people with disabilities or other employment barriers.

Hospice of Green Country
918-747-2273 www.hospiceofgreencountry.org
Provides compassionate and quality end-of-life care to patients and families regardless of ability to pay.

KIPP Tulsa College Preparatory
918-794-8652 www.kipptulsa.org

Provides middle school students with optimum academic and social skills to succeed in high school, college and a competitive world.

Legal Aid Services of Oklahoma
918-584-3338 www.legalaidok.org
Provides assistance to low-income and elderly persons with non-criminal legal issues.

LIFE Senior Services
918-664-9000 www.lifeseniorservices.org
Helps seniors and caregivers with a wide array of resources and services that promote independence, dignity and quality of life.

Margaret Hudson Program
918-833-9860 www.margarethudson.org
Provides education and support for pregnant teens including comprehensive academic, social and health services and child care.

Mental Health Association Oklahoma
918-585-1213 www.mhaok.org
Promotes mental health and mental disorder prevention through advocacy, education, housing and support services.

Morton Comprehensive Health Services
918-587-2171 www.mortonhealth.org
Provides quality, cost-effective and family-based health services with dignity and respect to all people without regard to finances, culture or lifestyle and provides information and support to promote participation in health care decisions.

Okmulgee County Family Resource Center
918-756-2549 http://www.okmulgeefrc.org/
Provides domestic violence intervention through emergency shelter, counseling/case management, and serves abused/neglected children.

Okmulgee County Homeless Shelter, Inc.
918-756-9098 www.okmulgeecountyhomelessshelter.org
Provides temporary emergency shelter, food, clothing and laundry facilities to move people from homelessness to self-sufficiency.

Okmulgee-Okfuskee County Youth Services
918-756-7700 www.annemoroneyyouthservices.com

Provides shelter, counseling, parenting, prevention education, truancy and advocacy programs for youth and families.

Operation Aware of Oklahoma, Inc.
918-582-7884 www.operationaware.org
Equips youth, through prevention education, with the knowledge and skills to make positive life choices.

Owasso Community Resources
918-272-4969 www.owassohelps.org
Provides basic needs assistance to financially disadvantaged residents of Owasso.

Palmer
918-832-7763 www.palmer-tulsa.org
Provides substance abuse outpatient treatment programs for adolescents and residential treatment for women and their children.

The Parent Child Center of Tulsa
918-599-7999 www.parentchildcenter.org
Strengthens families to break the cycle of child abuse and neglect through education, prevention, treatment and advocacy.

RSVP
918-280-8656 www.rsvptulsa.org
Enables senior volunteers to use their skills and time to help non-profit and public agencies in our community.

The Salvation Army
918-587-7801 www.salvationarmyaok.org
Provides shelter, transitional housing, case management, job readiness and emergency financial assistance for individuals and families. Also provides tutoring and educational programs, positive recreation and character development for youth, and support for families and seniors.

Sand Springs Community Services
918-245-5183 www.sscsok.org
Provides temporary/emergency relief by assisting clients with food, clothing, utility and rent payments.

Show, Inc.
918-224-7214 www.showinc.org
Provides services to people with developmental disabilities:
vocational/assisted living services to adults and respite care for
children.

Street School
918-833-9800 www.streetschool.org
A tuition-free dropout prevention program for students in grades 9 - 12
which includes education and therapeutic counseling.

Tristesse Grief Center
918-587-1200 www.thegriefcenter.org
Offers comprehensive, long-term grief counseling to assist the
bereaved as they journey toward improved health and a renewed
sense of worth in the wake of loss.

TSHA, Inc.
918-832-8742 www.tsha.cc
Provides interpreting, independent living and information and referral
services to encourage independence for those with hearing loss.

Tulsa Advocates for the Rights of Citizens with Developmental
Disabilities (TARC)
918-582-8272 www.ddadvocacy.net
Provides advocacy, education and support to people with
developmental disabilities and their families.

Tulsa Boys' Home
918-245-0231 www.tulsaboyshome.org
Provides residential treatment for adolescent males with mental
health, behavioral and substance abuse issues.

Tulsa CareS
918-834-4194 www.tulsacares.org
Delivers social services to low-income individuals living with

HIV/AIDS throughout northeastern Oklahoma.
Tulsa CASA, Tulsa Court Appointed Special Advocates
918-584-2272 www.tulsacasa.org

Trains community volunteers to advocate for the best interests of abused/neglected children in the Juvenile Court System of Tulsa County.

Tulsa Day Center for the Homeless
918-583-5588 www.tulsadaycenter.org
Provides daytime services for people who are homeless, such as shelter, restroom facilities, case management and a nurses' clinic.

Visiting Nurse Association of Tulsa
918-743-9810 www.vnaok.org
Provides home health care visits to those without Medicare, Medicaid, and/or third party health coverage.

Wagoner Area Neighbors
918-485-2309 www.wagonerhelps.org
Provides emergency food, financial assistance, clothing and information/referral services.

YMCA of Greater Tulsa
918-747-9622 www.ymcatulsa.org
Provides recreational, educational, health and child care programs for youth, adults and families.

Youth at Heart, Inc.
918-493-7311 www.youthatheart.org
Character building and crime prevention for at-risk youth through educational and recreational programs.

Youth Services of Creek County
918-227-2622 www.yscc.net
Provides crisis intervention, shelter and counseling programs for at-risk youth and families in Creek County.

Youth Services of Tulsa
918-582-0061 www.yst.org
Provides crisis services, counseling, skill building and positive development programs for adolescents.

YWCA Tulsa
918-587-2100 www.ywcatulsa.org

Eliminates racism and empowers women through counseling services, child and youth programs, immigration services and fitness training.

2-1-1* www.211tulsa.org
Call 2-1-1 Helpline 24/7 for information on crisis intervention services. Cell phones can reach the Helpline at 918-836-4357.
*A program of Community Service Council of Greater Tulsa.

School Districts & Phone

County	District Name	City	Phone
ADAIR	CAVE SPRINGS	Bunch	(918) 775-2364
ADAIR	GREASY	Bunch	(918) 696-7768
ADAIR	DAHLONEGAH	Stilwell	(918) 696-7807
ADAIR	MARYETTA	Stilwell	(918) 696-2285
ADAIR	PEAVINE	Stilwell	(918) 696-7818
ADAIR	ROCKY MOUNTAIN	Stilwell	(918) 696-7509
ADAIR	STILWELL	Stilwell	(918) 696-7001
ADAIR	ZION	Stilwell	(918) 696-7866
ADAIR	WATTS	Watts	(918) 422-5311
ADAIR	WESTVILLE	Westville	(918) 723-3181
ALFALFA	BURLINGTON	Burlington	(580) 431-2501
ALFALFA	CHEROKEE	Cherokee	(580) 596-3391
ALFALFA	TIMBERLAKE	Helena	(580) 852-3307
ATOKA	ATOKA	Atoka	(580) 889-6611
ATOKA	HARMONY	Atoka	(580) 889-3687
ATOKA	TUSHKA	Atoka	(580) 889-7355
ATOKA	CANEY	Caney	(580) 889-1996
ATOKA	LANE	Lane	(580) 889-2743
ATOKA	STRINGTOWN	Stringtown	(580) 346-7423
BEAVER	BALKO	Balko	(580) 646-3385
BEAVER	BEAVER	Beaver	(580) 625-3444
BEAVER	FORGAN	Forgan	(580) 487-3366
BEAVER	TURPIN	Turpin	(580) 778-3333
BECKHAM	ELK CITY	Elk City	(580) 225-0175
BECKHAM	MERRITT	Elk City	(580) 225-5460
BECKHAM	ERICK	Erick	(580) 526-3476
BECKHAM	SAYRE	Sayre	(580) 928-5531
BLAINE	CANTON	Canton	(580) 886-3516
BLAINE	GEARY	Geary	(405) 884-2989
BLAINE	OKEENE	Okeene	(580) 822-3268
BLAINE	WATONGA	Watonga	(580) 623-7364
BRYAN	ACHILLE	Achille	(580) 283-3775
BRYAN	BENNINGTON	Bennington	(580) 847-2737
BRYAN	ROCK CREEK	Bokchito	(580) 295-3137
BRYAN	CADDO	Caddo	(580) 367-2208

BRYAN	CALERA	Calera	(580) 434-5700
BRYAN	COLBERT	Colbert	(580) 296-2624
BRYAN	DURANT	Durant	(580) 924-1276
BRYAN	SILO	Durant	(580) 924-7000
CADDO	ANADARKO	Anadarko	(405) 247-6605
CADDO	BOONE-APACHE	Apache	(580) 588-3369
CADDO	BINGER-ONEY	Binger	(405) 656-2304
CADDO	CARNEGIE	Carnegie	(580) 654-1470
CADDO	CEMENT	Cement	(405) 489-3216
CADDO	CYRIL	Cyril	(580) 464-2419
CADDO	FORT COBB-BROXTON	Fort Cobb	(405) 643-2336
CADDO	GRACEMONT	Gracemont	(405) 966-2236
CADDO	HINTON	Hinton	(405) 542-3257
CADDO	HYDRO-EAKLY	Hydro	(405) 663-2774
CADDO	LOOKEBA SICKLES	Lookeba	(405) 457-6623
CANADIAN	CALUMET	Calumet	(405) 893-2222
CANADIAN	MAPLE	Calumet	(405) 262-5647
CANADIAN	BANNER	El Reno	(405) 262-0598
CANADIAN	DARLINGTON	El Reno	(405) 262-0137
CANADIAN	EL RENO	El Reno	(405) 262-1703
CANADIAN	RIVERSIDE	El Reno	(405) 262-2907
CANADIAN	MUSTANG	Mustang	(405) 376-2461
CANADIAN	PIEDMONT	Piedmont	(405) 373-2311
CANADIAN	UNION CITY	Union City	(405) 483-3531
CANADIAN	YUKON	Yukon	(405) 354-2587
CARTER	ARDMORE	Ardmore	(580) 226-7650
CARTER	DICKSON	Ardmore	(580) 223-9557
CARTER	PLAINVIEW	Ardmore	(580) 223-6319
CARTER	FOX	Fox	(580) 673-2081
CARTER	HEALDTON	Healdton	(580) 229-0566
CARTER	LONE GROVE	Lone Grove	(580) 657-3131
CARTER	SPRINGER	Springer	(580) 653-2656
CARTER	WILSON	Wilson	(580) 668-2306
CARTER	ZANEIS	Wilson	(580) 668-2955
CHEROKEE	HULBERT	Hulbert	(918) 772-2501
CHEROKEE	NORWOOD	Hulbert	(918) 478-3092
CHEROKEE	SHADY GROVE	Hulbert	(918) 772-2511
CHEROKEE	KEYS	Park Hill	(918) 458-1835

CHEROKEE	PEGGS	Peggs	(918) 598-3412
CHEROKEE	BRIGGS	Tahlequah	(918) 456-4221
CHEROKEE	GRAND VIEW	Tahlequah	(918) 456-5131
CHEROKEE	LOWREY	Tahlequah	(918) 456-4053
CHEROKEE	TAHLEQUAH	Tahlequah	(918) 458-4100
CHEROKEE	WOODALL	Tahlequah	(918) 458-5444
CHEROKEE	TENKILLER	Welling	(918) 457-5996
CHOCTAW	BOSWELL	Boswell	(580) 566-2558
CHOCTAW	FORT TOWSON	Fort Towson	(580) 873-2712
CHOCTAW	GRANT	Grant	(580) 326-8315
CHOCTAW	HUGO	Hugo	(580) 326-6483
CHOCTAW	SOPER	Soper	(580) 345-2757
CHOCTAW	SWINK	Swink	(580) 873-2695
CIMARRON	BOISE CITY	Boise City	(580) 544-3110
CIMARRON	FELT	Felt	(580) 426-2220
CIMARRON	KEYES	Keyes	(580) 546-7231
CLEVELAND	LEXINGTON	Lexington	(405) 527-7236
CLEVELAND	MOORE	Moore	(405) 735-4200
CLEVELAND	NOBLE	Noble	(405) 872-3452
CLEVELAND	LITTLE AXE	Norman	(405) 329-7691
CLEVELAND	NORMAN	Norman	(405) 364-1339
CLEVELAND	ROBIN HILL	Norman	(405) 321-4186
COAL	COALGATE	Coalgate	(580) 927-2351
COAL	COTTONWOOD	Coalgate	(580) 927-2937
COAL	TUPELO	Tupelo	(580) 845-2460
COMANCHE	CACHE	Cache	(580) 429-3266
COMANCHE	CHATTANOOGA	Chattanooga	(580) 597-3347
COMANCHE	ELGIN	Elgin	(580) 492-3663
COMANCHE	FLETCHER	Fletcher	(580) 549-3016
COMANCHE	GERONIMO	Geronimo	(580) 355-3160
COMANCHE	INDIAHOMA	Indiahoma	(580) 246-3448
COMANCHE	BISHOP	Lawton	(580) 353-4870
COMANCHE	FLOWER MOUND	Lawton	(580) 353-4088
COMANCHE	LAWTON	Lawton	(580) 357-6900
COMANCHE	STERLING	Sterling	(580) 365-4307
COTTON	BIG PASTURE	Randlett	(580) 281-3831
COTTON	TEMPLE	Temple	(580) 342-6230
COTTON	WALTERS	Walters	(580) 875-2568

CRAIG	BLUEJACKET	Bluejacket	(918) 784-2365
CRAIG	KETCHUM	Ketchum	(918) 782-5091
CRAIG	VINITA	Vinita	(918) 256-6778
CRAIG	WHITE OAK	Vinita	(918) 256-4484
CRAIG	WELCH	Welch	(918) 788-3129
CREEK	BRISTOW	Bristow	(918) 367-5555
CREEK	DEPEW	Depew	(918) 324-5466
CREEK	GYPSY	Depew	(918) 324-5365
CREEK	DRUMRIGHT	Drumright	(918) 352-2492
CREEK	OLIVE	Drumright	(918) 352-9567
CREEK	KELLYVILLE	Kellyville	(918) 247-6133
CREEK	KIEFER	Kiefer	(918) 321-3421
CREEK	MANNFORD	Mannford	(918) 865-4062
CREEK	MOUNDS	Mounds	(918) 827-6100
CREEK	OILTON	Oilton	(918) 862-3954
CREEK	LONE STAR	Sapulpa	(918) 224-0201
CREEK	PRETTY WATER	Sapulpa	(918) 224-4952
CREEK	SAPULPA	Sapulpa	(918) 224-3400
CREEK	ALLEN-BOWDEN	Tulsa	(918) 224-4440
CUSTER	ARAPAHO-BUTLER	Arapaho	(580) 323-3262
CUSTER	CLINTON	Clinton	(580) 323-1800
CUSTER	THOMAS-FAY-CUSTER UNIFIED DIST	Thomas	(580) 661-3527
CUSTER	WEATHERFORD	Weatherford	(580) 772-3327
DELAWARE	CLEORA	Afton	(918) 256-6401
DELAWARE	COLCORD	Colcord	(918) 326-4116
DELAWARE	MOSELEY	Colcord	(918) 422-5927
DELAWARE	GROVE	Grove	(918) 786-3003
DELAWARE	JAY	Jay	(918) 253-4293
DELAWARE	KANSAS	Kansas	(918) 868-2562
DELAWARE	OAKS-MISSION	Oaks	(918) 868-2183
DELAWARE	LEACH	Rose	(918) 868-2277
DELAWARE	KENWOOD	Salina	(918) 434-5799
DEWEY	SEILING	Seiling	(580) 922-7383
DEWEY	TALOGA	Taloga	(580) 328-5577
DEWEY	VICI	Vici	(580) 995-4744
ELLIS	ARNETT	Arnett	(580) 885-7811
ELLIS	FARGO	Fargo	(580) 698-2298

ELLIS	GAGE	Gage	(580) 923-7909
ELLIS	SHATTUCK	Shattuck	(580) 938-2586
GARFIELD	COVINGTON-DOUGLAS	Covington	(580) 864-7481
GARFIELD	DRUMMOND	Drummond	(580) 493-2216
GARFIELD	CHISHOLM	Enid	(580) 237-5512
GARFIELD	ENID	Enid	(580) 366-7000
GARFIELD	GARBER	Garber	(580) 863-2220
GARFIELD	KREMLIN-HILLSDALE	Kremlin	(580) 874-2284
GARFIELD	PIONEER-PLEASANT VALE	Waukomis	(580) 758-3282
GARFIELD	WAUKOMIS	Waukomis	(580) 758-3247
GARVIN	ELMORE CITY-PERNELL	Elmore City	(580) 788-2566
GARVIN	LINDSAY	Lindsay	(405) 756-3131
GARVIN	MAYSVILLE	Maysville	(888) 806-5220
GARVIN	PAOLI	Paoli	(405) 484-7336
GARVIN	PAULS VALLEY	Pauls Valley	(405) 238-6453
GARVIN	WHITEBEAD	Pauls Valley	(405) 238-3021
GARVIN	STRATFORD	Stratford	(580) 759-3615
GARVIN	WYNNEWOOD	Wynnewood	(405) 665-2004
GRADY	ALEX	Alex	(405) 785-2605
GRADY	AMBER-POCASSET	Amber	(405) 224-5768
GRADY	BRIDGE CREEK	Blanchard	(405) 387-4880
GRADY	MIDDLEBERG	Blanchard	(405) 485-3612
GRADY	CHICKASHA	Chickasha	(405) 222-6500
GRADY	FRIEND	Chickasha	(405) 224-3822
GRADY	PIONEER	Chickasha	(405) 224-2700
GRADY	MINCO	Minco	(405) 352-4867
GRADY	NINNEKAH	Ninnekah	(405) 224-4092
GRADY	RUSH SPRINGS	Rush Springs	(580) 476-3929
GRADY	TUTTLE	Tuttle	(405) 381-2605
GRADY	VERDEN	Verden	(405) 453-7247
GRANT	DEER CREEK-LAMONT	Lamont	(580) 388-4333
GRANT	MEDFORD	Medford	(580) 395-2392
GRANT	POND CREEK-HUNTER	Pond Creek	(580) 532-4242
GREER	GRANITE	Granite	(580) 535-2104
GREER	MANGUM	Mangum	(580) 782-3371
HARMON	HOLLIS	Hollis	(580) 688-3450
HARPER	BUFFALO	Buffalo	(580) 735-2448

HARPER	LAVERNE	Laverne	(580) 921-3362
HASKELL	KEOTA	Keota	(918) 966-3950
HASKELL	KINTA	Kinta	(918) 768-3338
HASKELL	MCCURTAIN	Mccurtain	(918) 945-7237
HASKELL	STIGLER	Stigler	(918) 967-2805
HASKELL	WHITEFIELD	Whitefield	(918) 967-8572
HUGHES	CALVIN	Calvin	(405) 645-2411
HUGHES	HOLDENVILLE	Holdenville	(405) 379-5483
HUGHES	MOSS	Holdenville	(405) 379-2273
HUGHES	STUART	Stuart	(918) 546-2476
HUGHES	WETUMKA	Wetumka	(405) 452-5150
JACKSON	ALTUS	Altus	(580) 481-2100
JACKSON	NAVAJO	Altus	(580) 482-7742
JACKSON	BLAIR	Blair	(580) 563-2632
JACKSON	DUKE	Duke	(580) 679-3014
JACKSON	ELDORADO	Eldorado	(580) 633-2219
JACKSON	OLUSTEE	Olustee	(580) 648-2243
JEFFERSON	RINGLING	Ringling	(580) 662-2385
JEFFERSON	RYAN	Ryan	(580) 757-2308
JEFFERSON	TERRAL	Terral	(580) 437-2244
JEFFERSON	WAURIKA	Waurika	(580) 228-3373
JOHNSTON	COLEMAN	Coleman	(580) 937-4418
JOHNSTON	MANNSVILLE	Mannsville	(580) 371-2892
JOHNSTON	MILBURN	Milburn	(580) 443-5522
JOHNSTON	MILL CREEK	Mill Creek	(580) 384-5514
JOHNSTON	RAVIA	Ravia	(580) 371-9163
JOHNSTON	TISHOMINGO	Tishomingo	(580) 371-9190
JOHNSTON	WAPANUCKA	Wapanucka	(580) 937-4466
KAY	BLACKWELL	Blackwell	(580) 363-2570
KAY	NEWKIRK	Newkirk	(580) 362-2388
KAY	PECKHAM	Newkirk	(580) 362-2633
KAY	KILDARE	Ponca City	(580) 362-2811
KAY	PONCA CITY	Ponca City	(580) 767-8000
KAY	TONKAWA	Tonkawa	(580) 628-3597
KINGFISHER	CASHION	Cashion	(405) 433-2741
KINGFISHER	DOVER	Dover	(405) 828-4206
KINGFISHER	HENNESSEY	Hennessey	(405) 853-4321
KINGFISHER	KINGFISHER	Kingfisher	(405) 375-4194

KINGFISHER	OKARCHE	Okarche	(405) 263-7300
KINGFISHER	LOMEGA	Omega	(405) 729-4215
KIOWA	HOBART	Hobart	(580) 726-5691
KIOWA	LONE WOLF	Lone Wolf	(580) 846-9091
KIOWA	MOUNTAIN VIEW-GOTEBO	Mountain View	(580) 347-2211
KIOWA	SNYDER	Snyder	(580) 569-2773
LATIMER	RED OAK	Red Oak	(918) 754-2426
LATIMER	BUFFALO VALLEY	Talihina	(918) 522-4426
LATIMER	PANOLA	Wilburton	(918) 465-3298
LATIMER	WILBURTON	Wilburton	(918) 465-2100
LE FLORE	ARKOMA	Arkoma	(918) 875-3351
LE FLORE	BOKOSHE	Bokoshe	(918) 969-2491
LE FLORE	CAMERON	Cameron	(918) 654-3225
LE FLORE	FANSHAWE	Fanshawe	(918) 659-2341
LE FLORE	HEAVENER	Heavener	(918) 653-7223
LE FLORE	HODGEN	Hodgen	(918) 653-4476
LE FLORE	HOWE	Howe	(918) 658-3666
LE FLORE	LE FLORE	Leflore	(918) 753-2345
LE FLORE	MONROE	Monroe	(918) 658-3516
LE FLORE	PANAMA	Panama	(918) 963-2217
LE FLORE	POCOLA	Pocola	(918) 436-2424
LE FLORE	POTEAU	Poteau	(918) 647-7700
LE FLORE	SHADY POINT	Shady Point	(918) 963-2595
LE FLORE	SPIRO	Spiro	(918) 962-2463
LE FLORE	TALIHINA	Talihina	(918) 567-2259
LE FLORE	WHITESBORO	Whitesboro	(918) 567-2556
LE FLORE	WISTER	Wister	(918) 655-7381
LINCOLN	AGRA	Agra	(918) 375-2261
LINCOLN	CARNEY	Carney	(405) 865-2344
LINCOLN	CHANDLER	Chandler	(405) 258-1450
LINCOLN	DAVENPORT	Davenport	(918) 377-2277
LINCOLN	WHITE ROCK	Mcloud	(405) 964-3428
LINCOLN	MEEKER	Meeker	(405) 279-3511
LINCOLN	PRAGUE	Prague	(405) 567-4455
LINCOLN	STROUD	Stroud	(918) 968-2541
LINCOLN	WELLSTON	Wellston	(405) 356-2534
LOGAN	COYLE	Coyle	(405) 466-2242

LOGAN	CRESCENT	Crescent	(405) 969-3738
LOGAN	GUTHRIE	Guthrie	(405) 282-8900
LOGAN	MULHALL-ORLANDO	Orlando	(405) 649-2000
LOVE	TURNER	Burneyville	(580) 276-1307
LOVE	GREENVILLE	Marietta	(580) 276-2968
LOVE	MARIETTA	Marietta	(580) 276-9444
LOVE	THACKERVILLE	Thackerville	(580) 276-2630
MAJOR	ALINE-CLEO	Aline	(580) 463-2255
MAJOR	FAIRVIEW	Fairview	(580) 227-2531
MAJOR	CIMARRON	Lahoma	(580) 796-2204
MAJOR	RINGWOOD	Ringwood	(580) 883-2202
MARSHALL	KINGSTON	Kingston	(580) 564-9033
MARSHALL	MADILL	Madill	(580) 795-3303
MAYES	ADAIR	Adair	(918) 785-2424
MAYES	CHOUTEAU-MAZIE	Chouteau	(918) 476-8376
MAYES	LOCUST GROVE	Locust Grove	(918) 479-5243
MAYES	OSAGE	Pryor	(918) 825-2550
MAYES	PRYOR	Pryor	(918) 825-1255
MAYES	SALINA	Salina	(918) 434-5091
MAYES	WICKLIFFE	Salina	(918) 434-5558
MAYES	SPAVINAW	Spavinaw	(918) 589-2228
MCCLAIN	BLANCHARD	Blanchard	(405) 485-3391
MCCLAIN	DIBBLE	Blanchard	(405) 344-6375
MCCLAIN	BYARS	Byars	(405) 783-4366
MCCLAIN	NEWCASTLE	Newcastle	(405) 387-2890
MCCLAIN	PURCELL	Purcell	(405) 527-2146
MCCLAIN	WASHINGTON	Washington	(405) 288-6190
MCCLAIN	WAYNE	Wayne	(405) 449-3646
MCCURTAIN	BATTIEST	Broken Bow	(580) 241-7810
MCCURTAIN	BROKEN BOW	Broken Bow	(580) 584-3306
MCCURTAIN	GLOVER	Broken Bow	(580) 420-3232
MCCURTAIN	HOLLY CREEK	Broken Bow	(580) 420-6961
MCCURTAIN	LUKFATA	Broken Bow	(580) 584-6834
MCCURTAIN	EAGLETOWN	Eagletown	(580) 835-2242
MCCURTAIN	FOREST GROVE	Garvin	(580) 286-3961
MCCURTAIN	HAWORTH	Haworth	(580) 245-1406
MCCURTAIN	DENISON	Idabel	(580) 286-3319
MCCURTAIN	IDABEL	Idabel	(580) 286-7639

MCCURTAIN	SMITHVILLE	Smithville	(580) 244-3333
MCCURTAIN	VALLIANT	Valliant	(580) 933-7232
MCCURTAIN	WRIGHT CITY	Wright City	(580) 981-2824
MCINTOSH	CHECOTAH	Checotah	(918) 473-5610
MCINTOSH	MIDWAY	Council Hill	(918) 474-3434
MCINTOSH	EUFAULA	Eufaula	(918) 689-2152
MCINTOSH	STIDHAM	Eufaula	(918) 689-5241
MCINTOSH	HANNA	Hanna	(918) 657-2523
MCINTOSH	RYAL	Henryetta	(918) 652-7461
MURRAY	DAVIS	Davis	(580) 369-2386
MURRAY	SULPHUR	Sulphur	(580) 622-2061
MUSKOGEE	BRAGGS	Braggs	(918) 487-5265
MUSKOGEE	FORT GIBSON	Fort Gibson	(918) 478-2474
MUSKOGEE	HASKELL	Haskell	(918) 482-5221
MUSKOGEE	HILLDALE	Muskogee	(918) 683-0273
MUSKOGEE	MUSKOGEE	Muskogee	(918) 684-3700
MUSKOGEE	OKTAHA	Oktaha	(918) 687-7556
MUSKOGEE	PORUM	Porum	(918) 484-5121
MUSKOGEE	WAINWRIGHT	Wainwright	(918) 474-3484
MUSKOGEE	WARNER	Warner	(918) 463-5171
MUSKOGEE	WEBBERS FALLS	Webbers Falls	(918) 464-2334
NOBLE	BILLINGS	Billings	(580) 725-3271
NOBLE	MORRISON	Morrison	(580) 724-3341
NOBLE	PERRY	Perry	(580) 336-4511
NOBLE	FRONTIER	Red Rock	(580) 723-4361
NOWATA	NOWATA	Nowata	(918) 273-3425
NOWATA	OKLAHOMA UNION	South Coffeyville	(918) 255-6550
NOWATA	SOUTH COFFEYVILLE	South Coffeyville	(918) 255-6202
OKFUSKEE	MASON	Mason	(918) 623-0231
OKFUSKEE	BEARDEN	Okemah	(918) 623-0156
OKFUSKEE	OKEMAH	Okemah	(918) 623-1874
OKFUSKEE	GRAHAM-DUSTIN CHARTER: EPIC	Oklahoma City	(405) 749-4550
OKFUSKEE	PADEN	Paden	(405) 932-5053
OKFUSKEE	GRAHAM-DUSTIN	Weleetka	(918) 652-8935
OKFUSKEE	WELEETKA	Weleetka	(405) 786-2203

OKLAHOMA	BETHANY	Bethany	(405) 789-3801
OKLAHOMA	CHOCTAW-NICOMA PARK	Choctaw	(405) 769-4859
OKLAHOMA	DEER CREEK	Edmond	(405) 348-6100
OKLAHOMA	EDMOND	Edmond	(405) 340-2828
OKLAHOMA	OAKDALE	Edmond	(405) 771-3373
OKLAHOMA	HARRAH	Harrah	(405) 454-6244
OKLAHOMA	JONES	Jones	(405) 399-9215
OKLAHOMA	LUTHER	Luther	(405) 277-3233
OKLAHOMA	MIDWEST CITY-DEL CITY	Midwest City	(405) 737-4461
OKLAHOMA	CHOCTAW-NICOMA PARK CHARTER	Nicoma Park	(405) 259-9478
OKLAHOMA	OKC CHARTER: SANTA FE SOUTH HS	Ok City	(405) 631-6100
OKLAHOMA	OKC CHARTER: SEEWORTH ACADEMY	Okc	(405) 475-6400
OKLAHOMA	CROOKED OAK	Oklahoma City	(405) 677-5252
OKLAHOMA	CRUTCHO	Oklahoma City	(405) 427-3771
OKLAHOMA	MILLWOOD	Oklahoma City	(405) 478-1336
OKLAHOMA	OKC CHARTER: ASTEC CHARTERS	Oklahoma City	(405) 947-6272
OKLAHOMA	OKC CHARTER: DOVE SCIENCE ACAD	Oklahoma City	(405) 524-9762
OKLAHOMA	OKC CHARTER: DOVE SCIENCE ES	Oklahoma City	(405) 605-5566
OKLAHOMA	OKC CHARTER: HARDING CHARTER	Oklahoma City	(405) 528-0562
OKLAHOMA	OKC CHARTER: HARDING FINE ARTS	Oklahoma City	(405) 702-4322
OKLAHOMA	OKC CHARTER: HARPER ACADEMY	Oklahoma City	(405) 605-2600
OKLAHOMA	OKC CHARTER: HUPFELD/W VILLAGE	Oklahoma City	(405) 751-1774
OKLAHOMA	OKC CHARTER: INDEPENDENCE MS	Oklahoma City	(405) 767-3000
OKLAHOMA	OKC CHARTER: KIPP REACH COLL	Oklahoma City	(405) 425-4622
OKLAHOMA	OKC CHARTER: SANTA FE SOUTH MS	Oklahoma City	(405) 635-1053
OKLAHOMA	OKLAHOMA CITY	Oklahoma City	(405) 587-0000
OKLAHOMA	WESTERN HEIGHTS	Oklahoma City	(405) 350-3410

OKLAHOMA	PUTNAM CITY	Warr Acres	(405) 495-5200
OKMULGEE	BEGGS	Beggs	(918) 267-3628
OKMULGEE	DEWAR	Dewar	(918) 652-9625
OKMULGEE	HENRYETTA	Henryetta	(918) 652-6523
OKMULGEE	WILSON	Henryetta	(918) 652-3374
OKMULGEE	MORRIS	Morris	(918) 733-9072
OKMULGEE	OKMULGEE	Okmulgee	(918) 758-2000
OKMULGEE	TWIN HILLS	Okmulgee	(918) 733-2531
OKMULGEE	PRESTON	Preston	(918) 756-3388
OKMULGEE	SCHULTER	Schulter	(918) 652-8219
OSAGE	AVANT	Avant	(918) 263-2135
OSAGE	BARNSDALL	Barnsdall	(918) 847-2271
OSAGE	OSAGE HILLS	Bartlesville	(918) 336-6804
OSAGE	WOODLAND	Fairfax	(918) 642-3297
OSAGE	HOMINY	Hominy	(918) 885-6511
OSAGE	BOWRING	Pawhuska	(918) 336-6892
OSAGE	PAWHUSKA	Pawhuska	(918) 287-1265
OSAGE	MCCORD	Ponca City	(580) 765-8806
OSAGE	PRUE	Prue	(918) 242-3351
OSAGE	ANDERSON	Sand Springs	(918) 245-0289
OSAGE	SHIDLER	Shidler	(918) 793-2021
OSAGE	WYNONA	Wynona	(918) 846-2467
OTTAWA	AFTON	Afton	(918) 257-8303
OTTAWA	COMMERCE	Commerce	(918) 675-4316
OTTAWA	FAIRLAND	Fairland	(918) 676-3811
OTTAWA	MIAMI	Miami	(918) 542-8455
OTTAWA	QUAPAW	Quapaw	(918) 674-2501
OTTAWA	TURKEY FORD	Wyandotte	(918) 786-4902
OTTAWA	WYANDOTTE	Wyandotte	(918) 678-2255
PAWNEE	CLEVELAND	Cleveland	(918) 358-2210
PAWNEE	JENNINGS	Jennings	(918) 757-2536
PAWNEE	PAWNEE	Pawnee	(918) 762-3676
PAYNE	CUSHING	Cushing	(918) 225-3425
PAYNE	OAK GROVE	Cushing	(918) 352-2889
PAYNE	GLENCOE	Glencoe	(580) 669-4003
PAYNE	PERKINS-TRYON	Perkins	(405) 547-5703
PAYNE	RIPLEY	Ripley	(918) 372-4567
PAYNE	STILLWATER	Stillwater	(405) 533-6300

PAYNE	YALE	Yale	(918) 387-2434
PITTSBURG	CANADIAN	Canadian	(918) 339-7251
PITTSBURG	CROWDER	Crowder	(918) 334-3203
PITTSBURG	HAILEYVILLE	Haileyville	(918) 297-2626
PITTSBURG	HARTSHORNE	Hartshorne	(918) 297-2534
PITTSBURG	INDIANOLA	Indianola	(918) 823-4231
PITTSBURG	KIOWA	Kiowa	(918) 432-5631
PITTSBURG	KREBS	Krebs	(918) 426-4700
PITTSBURG	FRINK-CHAMBERS	Mcalester	(918) 423-2434
PITTSBURG	HAYWOOD	Mcalester	(918) 423-6265
PITTSBURG	MCALESTER	Mcalester	(918) 423-4771
PITTSBURG	TANNEHILL	Mcalester	(918) 423-6393
PITTSBURG	PITTSBURG	Pittsburg	(918) 432-5062
PITTSBURG	QUINTON	Quinton	(918) 469-3100
PITTSBURG	SAVANNA	Savanna	(918) 548-3777
PONTOTOC	ADA	Ada	(580) 310-7200
PONTOTOC	BYNG	Ada	(580) 310-6751
PONTOTOC	LATTA	Ada	(580) 332-2092
PONTOTOC	VANOSS	Ada	(580) 759-2251
PONTOTOC	ALLEN	Allen	(580) 857-2417
PONTOTOC	ROFF	Roff	(580) 456-7663
PONTOTOC	STONEWALL	Stonewall	(580) 265-4241
POTTAWATOMIE	ASHER	Asher	(405) 784-2331
POTTAWATOMIE	DALE	Dale	(405) 964-5558
POTTAWATOMIE	EARLSBORO	Earlsboro	(405) 997-5616
POTTAWATOMIE	MACOMB	Macomb	(405) 598-3892
POTTAWATOMIE	MAUD	Maud	(405) 374-2416
POTTAWATOMIE	MCLOUD	Mcloud	(405) 964-3314
POTTAWATOMIE	BETHEL	Shawnee	(405) 273-0385
POTTAWATOMIE	GROVE	Shawnee	(405) 275-7435
POTTAWATOMIE	NORTH ROCK CREEK	Shawnee	(405) 275-3473
POTTAWATOMIE	PLEASANT GROVE	Shawnee	(405) 275-6092
POTTAWATOMIE	SHAWNEE	Shawnee	(405) 273-0653
POTTAWATOMIE	SOUTH ROCK CREEK	Shawnee	(405) 273-6072
POTTAWATOMIE	TECUMSEH	Tecumseh	(405) 598-3739
POTTAWATOMIE	WANETTE	Wanette	(405) 383-2656
PUSHMATAHA	ALBION	Albion	(918) 563-4331
PUSHMATAHA	ANTLERS	Antlers	(580) 298-5504

PUSHMATAHA	CLAYTON	Clayton	(918) 569-4492
PUSHMATAHA	MOYERS	Moyers	(580) 298-5549
PUSHMATAHA	NASHOBA	Nashoba	(918) 755-4343
PUSHMATAHA	RATTAN	Rattan	(580) 587-2546
PUSHMATAHA	TUSKAHOMA	Tuskahoma	(918) 569-7737
ROGER MILLS	CHEYENNE	Cheyenne	(580) 497-3371
ROGER MILLS	HAMMON	Hammon	(580) 473-2221
ROGER MILLS	LEEDEY	Leedey	(580) 488-3424
ROGER MILLS	REYDON	Reydon	(580) 655-4375
ROGER MILLS	SWEETWATER	Sweetwater	(580) 534-2272
ROGERS	CATOOSA	Catoosa	(918) 266-8603
ROGERS	CHELSEA	Chelsea	(918) 789-2528
ROGERS	CLAREMORE	Claremore	(918) 923-4200
ROGERS	JUSTUS-TIAWAH	Claremore	(918) 341-3626
ROGERS	SEQUOYAH	Claremore	(918) 341-5472
ROGERS	VERDIGRIS	Claremore	(918) 266-7227
ROGERS	FOYIL	Foyil	(918) 341-1113
ROGERS	INOLA	Inola	(918) 543-2255
ROGERS	OOLOGAH-TALALA	Oologah	(918) 443-6079
SEMINOLE	BOWLEGS	Bowlegs	(405) 398-4172
SEMINOLE	BUTNER	Cromwell	(405) 944-5530
SEMINOLE	KONAWA	Konawa	(580) 925-3244
SEMINOLE	SASAKWA	Sasakwa	(405) 941-3250
SEMINOLE	SEMINOLE	Seminole	(405) 382-5085
SEMINOLE	STROTHER	Seminole	(405) 382-4014
SEMINOLE	VARNUM	Seminole	(405) 382-1448
SEMINOLE	JUSTICE	Wewoka	(405) 257-2962
SEMINOLE	NEW LIMA	Wewoka	(405) 257-5771
SEMINOLE	WEWOKA	Wewoka	(405) 257-5475
SEQUOYAH	MARBLE CITY	Bunch	(918) 775-2135
SEQUOYAH	GANS	Gans	(918) 775-2236
SEQUOYAH	GORE	Gore	(918) 489-5587
SEQUOYAH	MOFFETT	Moffett	(918) 875-3668
SEQUOYAH	BELFONTE	Muldrow	(918) 427-3522
SEQUOYAH	LIBERTY	Muldrow	(918) 427-3808
SEQUOYAH	MULDROW	Muldrow	(918) 427-7406
SEQUOYAH	ROLAND	Roland	(918) 427-4601
SEQUOYAH	BRUSHY	Sallisaw	(918) 775-4458

SEQUOYAH	CENTRAL	Sallisaw	(918) 775-5525
SEQUOYAH	SALLISAW	Sallisaw	(918) 775-5544
SEQUOYAH	VIAN	Vian	(918) 773-5798
STEPHENS	COMANCHE	Comanche	(580) 439-2900
STEPHENS	GRANDVIEW	Comanche	(580) 439-2467
STEPHENS	DUNCAN	Duncan	(580) 255-0686
STEPHENS	EMPIRE	Duncan	(580) 252-5392
STEPHENS	BRAY-DOYLE	Marlow	(580) 658-5076
STEPHENS	CENTRAL HIGH	Marlow	(580) 658-6858
STEPHENS	MARLOW	Marlow	(580) 658-2719
STEPHENS	VELMA-ALMA	Velma	(580) 444-3355
TEXAS	GOODWELL	Goodwell	(580) 349-2271
TEXAS	YARBROUGH	Goodwell	(580) 545-3327
TEXAS	GUYMON	Guymon	(580) 338-4340
TEXAS	STRAIGHT	Guymon	(580) 652-2232
TEXAS	HARDESTY	Hardesty	(580) 888-4258
TEXAS	HOOKER	Hooker	(580) 652-2162
TEXAS	OPTIMA	Optima	(580) 338-6712
TEXAS	TEXHOMA	Texhoma	(580) 423-7433
TEXAS	TYRONE	Tyrone	(580) 854-6298
TILLMAN	DAVIDSON	Davidson	(580) 568-2423
TILLMAN	FREDERICK	Frederick	(580) 335-5516
TILLMAN	GRANDFIELD	Grandfield	(580) 479-5237
TILLMAN	TIPTON	Tipton	(580) 667-5268
TULSA	BIXBY	Bixby	(918) 366-2200
TULSA	BROKEN ARROW	Broken Arrow	(918) 259-5700
TULSA	COLLINSVILLE	Collinsville	(918) 371-2326
TULSA	GLENPOOL	Glenpool	(918) 322-9500
TULSA	JENKS	Jenks	(918) 299-4411
TULSA	LIBERTY	Mounds	(918) 366-8496
TULSA	OWASSO	Owasso	(918) 272-5367
TULSA	KEYSTONE	Sand Springs	(918) 363-8711
TULSA	SAND SPRINGS	Sand Springs	(918) 246-1400
TULSA	SKIATOOK	Skiatook	(918) 396-1792
TULSA	SPERRY	Sperry	(918) 288-6258
TULSA	BERRYHILL	Tulsa	(918) 446-1966
TULSA	TULSA	Tulsa	(918) 746-6800

TULSA	TULSA CHARTER: KIPP TULSA	Tulsa	(918) 794-8652
TULSA	TULSA CHARTER: LIGHTHOUSE ACAD	Tulsa	(918) 794-1442
TULSA	TULSA CHARTER: SCHL ARTS/SCI	Tulsa	(918) 828-7727
TULSA	UNION	Tulsa	(918) 357-4321
WAGONER	COWETA	Coweta	(918) 486-6506
WAGONER	OKAY	Okay	(918) 682-2548
WAGONER	PORTER CONSOLIDATED	Porter	(918) 483-2401
WAGONER	WAGONER	Wagoner	(918) 485-4046
WASHINGTON	BARTLESVILLE	Bartlesville	(918) 336-8600
WASHINGTON	COPAN	Copan	(918) 532-4490
WASHINGTON	DEWEY	Dewey	(918) 534-2241
WASHINGTON	CANEY VALLEY	Ramona	(918) 536-2500
WASHITA	BURNS FLAT-DILL CITY	Burns Flat	(580) 562-4844
WASHITA	CANUTE	Canute	(580) 472-3295
WASHITA	CORDELL	Cordell	(580) 832-3420
WASHITA	SENTINEL	Sentinel	(580) 393-2101
WOODS	ALVA	Alva	(580) 327-4823
WOODS	FREEDOM	Freedom	(580) 621-3271
WOODS	WAYNOKA	Waynoka	(580) 824-6561
WOODWARD	FORT SUPPLY	Fort Supply	(580) 766-2611
WOODWARD	MOORELAND	Mooreland	(580) 994-5388
WOODWARD	SHARON-MUTUAL	Mutual	(580) 989-3210
WOODWARD	WOODWARD	Woodward	(580) 256-6063

State Agencies

Governor Mary Fallin
(405) 521-2342

Oklahoma Tax
Commission
(405) 521-3160

Oklahoma Board of
Nursing
(405) 962-1800

Oklahoma State Board of
Pharmacy
(405) 521-3815

Oklahoma Board of
Medical Licensure and
Supervision
(405) 962-1400

Oklahoma ABLE
Commission
(405) 521-3484

Oklahoma Department of
Human Services
(405) 521-3646

Oklahoma Department of
Public Safety (405) 425-
2424

Division of Capital Assets
Management
(405) 521-2121

Office of Personnel
anagement
(405) 521-2177

Oklahoma Real Estate
Commission
(405) 521-3387

Oklahoma Secretary of
State
(405) 521-3912

Oklahoma State Board of
Osteopathic Examiners
(405) 528-8625

Oklahoma Bureau of
Narcotics and Dangerous
Drugs Control
(405) 521-2885

Oklahoma Employment
Security Commission
(405) 557-7200

The Author

Thank you for your support!

My name is Purin Williams, Director for Make A' Move Housing Association. I've served our community in the housing industry for the last 15 years. Make A Move Housing Association was started to help solve the more complex barriers to homeownership. Our pro-active leadership and strategic partnerships allow us to help meet the needs of  the community and our partners in a cost-effective and efficient manner. We promote organizations that share our values of serving the public with dignity, compassion and respect. Our community is facing real challenges in bridging the information gap among low to moderate income wage earners.

It is my sole purpose to make this guide available to assist those helping others to help themselves. According to a recent report released by the Health and Service Administration, the #1 reason for system poverty is the lack of information. When you share these materials with those you serve you too participate in the fight to eliminate systemic poverty.

Purin Williams, Director
Make A' Move Housing Association
williams@makeamovehousing.org

Prayer of Salvation:

Your Father God wants to have a relationship with you. He's been in your life since birth, but it's been difficult to communicate with you.

He needs you to receive His gift of salvation for you and your household to be saved from the destruction that is to come.

From creation he had a plan to bring you back to him. This plan had to be done by God sending His Son Jesus Christ to absorb you of sin. You are forgiven from your Sin right now. Your salvation was settled when God raised Jesus from the dead. God is a gentlemen and will never force himself on you. He's waiting on you to accept Him in your life by receiving the gift of salvation through Jesus.

You've tried everything and have found no relief. If your heart compels you, I urge you to pray the following prayer.

According to the scripture in Romans 10:9-13New Living Translation (NLT)- 9 If you openly declare that Jesus is Lord and believe in your heart that God raised him from the dead, you will be saved. 10 For it is by believing in your heart that you are made right with God, and it is by openly declaring your faith that you are saved. 11 As the Scriptures tell us, "Anyone who trusts in him will never be disgraced."[a] 12 Jew and Gentile[b] are the same in this respect. They have the same Lord, who gives generously to all who call on him. 13 For "Everyone who calls on the name of the Lord will be saved."[c]

Pray a prayer like this:

Dear God I call upon the name of Jesus. I accept that he is your Son and that you raised him from the dead. If there be any doubt in my heart that you raised him from the dead, I ask you to help me to believe.

I openly declare that Jesus is my Lord and I believe in my heart that God has raised him from the dead therefore, I am saved from the penalty of Sin. Thank you for helping me. I trust you to do as the scripture says in Romans 10:9-13 and save me. In Jesus Name I pray, Amen.

I urge you to:

- Read Matthew, Mark, Luke, and John in the Holy Bible
- Tell someone that you have accepted Jesus as Lord
- Ask the Father to lead you to a church home
- Share your salvation with others.

Your New Life:

Jesus Christ is the Son of God, born of a virgin to die on the cross for our sins. The Bible tells us that he walked on the earth and did not sin. When you read Matthew, Mark, Luke and John in the Holy Bible you will get to know him.

Jesus teaches us how to interact with God and that we are children of God. Before Jesus came we could only gain access to God by performing sacrifices that would take the place of our sin. Jesus came to replace the law that made us guilty before God. It is because of His sacrifice we can stand innocent before God.

Once we believe that Jesus is our Savior we are saved from eternal soul damnation and we spend our life in Heaven after we depart earth. We live our life in Christ, similar to how a wife lives her life in the husband. The wife takes the husbands name and becomes one with him. **Once you accept Jesus as your Savior you are now called Righteous and every time you see that word in the Bible it applies to you.** The Father will answer your prayer based on His Son's record (which is free from any wrongdoing) and not yours.

- If you read or hear any message that tells you that you owe anything for this gift of salvation, reject it immediately.

- Please be patient as the Love of God helps you to walk-in a freedom you've never experienced before.

My Prayer For You:

I pray that the Love of my Father and Power of his Holy Spirit gently guide and teach you concerning all things. May his face shine upon you and his angels surround you to keep you safe in all you do. In the name of my Lord and Savior Jesus Christ I Pray, Amen.

Guarantee

But my God shall supply all your need according to his riches in glory by Christ Jesus. Philippians 4:19

Addictions

- And call upon me in the day of trouble: I will deliver thee, and thou shalt glorify me. - Psalms 50:15

- The Spirit of the Lord God is upon me; because the Lord hath anointed me to preach good tidings unto the meek; he hath sent me to bind up the brokenhearted, to proclaim liberty to the captives, and the opening of the prison to them that are bound; - Isaiah 61:1

- A new heart also will I give you, and a new Spirit will I put within you: and I will take away the stony heart out of your flesh, and I will give you and heart of flesh. And I will put my Spirit within you, and cause you to walk-in my statutes, and ye shall keep my judgments, and do them. - Ezekiel 36:26-27

- If the Son therefore shall make you free, ye shall be free indeed.- John 8:36

- There is therefore now no condemnation to them which are in Christ Jesus, who walk not after the flesh, but after the Spirit. For the law of the Spirit of life in Christ Jesus hath made me free from the law of sin and death.- Romans 8:1-2

- There hath no temptation taken you but such as is common to man: but God is faithful, who will not suffer you to be tempted above that ye are able; but will with the temptation also make a way to escape, that ye may be able to bear it. 1 Corinthians 10:13

- Therefore, if any man be in Christ, he is a new creature: old things are passed away; behold, all things are become new.2 Corinthians 5:17

Deliverance From Harassment

- The angel of the Lord encamped round about them that fear him, and delivered them. Psalms 34:7

- For thou hast been a shelter for me, and a strong tower from the enemy.Psalms 61:3

- Because he hath set his Love upon me, therefore will I deliver him: I will set him on high, because he hath known my name. He shall call upon me, and I will answer him: I will be with him in trouble; I will deliver him, and honor him. Psalms 91:14-15

- And Jesus rebuked the devil; and he departed out of him: and the child was cured from that very hour. Then came the disciples to Jesus apart, and said, why could not we cast him out? And Jesus said unto them, Because of your unbelief: for verily I say unto you, if ye have faith as a grain of mustard seed, ye shall say unto this mountain, Remove hence to yonder place; and it shall remove; and nothing shall be impossible unto you. Howbeit this kind goeth not out but by prayer and fasting.
  - Matthew 17:18-21

- And Jesus returned in the power of the Spirit into Galilee: and there went out a fame of him through all the region round about. And he taught in their synagogues, being glorified of all. And he came to Nazareth, where he had been brought up: and, as his custom was, he went into the synagogue on the Sabbath day, and stood up for to read. And there was delivered unto him the book of the prophet Esaias. And when he had opened the book, he found the place where it was written, The Spirit of the Lord is upon me, because he hath anointed me to preach the gospel to the poor; he hath sent me to heal the brokenhearted, to preach deliverance to the captives, and recovering of sight to the blind, to set at liberty them that are bruised,- Luke 4:14-18

- Submit yourselves therefore to God. Resist the devil, and he will flee from you. James 4:7

- And I heard a loud voice saying in Heaven, now is come salvation, and strength, and the kingdom of our God, and the power of his Christ: for the accuser of our brethren is cast down, which accused them before our God day and night. And they overcame him by the blood of the Lamb, and by the word of their testimony; and they loved not their lives unto the death.- Revelation 12:10-11

Depression

- The Lord also will be a refuge for the oppressed, a refuge in times of trouble. And they that know thy name will put their trust in thee: for thou, Lord, hast not forsaken them that seek thee.- Psalms 9:9-10

- The Righteous cry, and the Lord heareth, and delivereth them out of all their troubles.- Psalms 34:17

- Then they cried unto the Lord in their trouble, and he saved them out of their distresses. He brought them out of darkness and the shadow of death, and brake their bands in sunder. Oh that men would praise the Lord for his goodness, and for his wonderful works to the children of men! For he hath broken the gates of brass, and cut the bars of iron in sunder.- Psalms 107:13-16

- Heaviness in the heart of man maketh it stoop: but a good word maketh it glad. Proverbs 12:25

- Fear thou not; for I am with thee: be not dismayed; for I am thy God: I will strengthen thee; yea, I will help thee; yea, I will uphold thee with the right hand of my righteousness.- Isaiah 41:10

- For the mountains shall depart, and the hills be removed; but my kindness shall not depart from thee, neither shall the covenant of my peace be removed, saith the Lord that hath mercy on thee.- Isaiah 54:10

- Remembering mine affliction and my misery, the wormwood and the gall. My soul hath them still in remembrance, and is humbled in me. This I recall to my mind, therefore have I hope. It is of the Lord's mercies that we are not consumed, because his compassions fail not. They are new every morning: great is thy faithfulness. The Lord is my portion, saith my soul; therefore will I hope in him. The Lord is good unto them that wait for him, to the soul that seeketh him.- Lamentations 3:19-25

- Grace be to you and peace from God our Father, and from the Lord Jesus Christ. Blessed be God, even the Father of our Lord Jesus Christ, the Father of mercies, and the God of all comfort; Who comforted us in all our tribulation, that we may be able to comfort them which are in any trouble, by the comfort wherewith we ourselves are comforted of God. - 2 Corinthians 1:2-4

Family

- But the mercy of the Lord is from everlasting to everlasting upon them that fear him, and his righteousness unto children's children;- Psalms 103:17

- The Father of the Righteous shall greatly rejoice: and he that begetteth a wise child shall have joy of him.- Proverbs 23:24

- For I will pour water upon him that is thirsty, and floods upon the dry ground: I will pour my Spirit upon thy seed, and my blessing upon thine offspring:- Isaiah 44:3

- But thus saith the Lord, Even the captives of the mighty shall be taken away, and the prey of the terrible shall be delivered: for I will contend with him that contended with thee, and I will save thy children.- Isaiah 49:25

- And he shall turn the heart of the fathers to the children, and the heart of the children to their fathers...- Malachi 4:6

Fear

- The Lord shall fight for you, and ye shall hold your peace.- Exodus 14:14

- And the Lord, he it is that doth go before thee; he will be with thee, he will not fail thee, neither forsake thee: fear not, neither be dismayed.- Deuteronomy 31:8

- Have not I commanded thee? Be strong and of a good courage; be not afraid, neither be thou dismayed: for the Lord thy God is with thee whithersoever thou goest.- Joshua 1:9

- I will call upon the Lord, who is worthy to be praised: so shall I be saved from mine enemies.- Psalms 18:3

- Yea, though I walk through the valley of the shadow of death, I will fear no evil: for thou art with me; thy rod and thy staff they comfort me.- Psalms 23:4

- The Lord is my light and my salvation; whom shall I fear? the Lord is the strength of my life; of whom shall I be afraid?- Psalms 27:1

- The angel of the Lord encamped round about them that fear him, and delivereth them.- Psalms 34:7

- For thou hast been a shelter for me, and a strong tower from the enemy.- Psalms 61:3

- For I the Lord thy God will hold thy right hand, saying unto thee, Fear not; I will help thee.- Isaiah 41:13

- When thou passest through the waters, I will be with thee; and through the rivers, they shall not overflow thee: when thou walkest through the fire, thou shalt not be burned; neither shall the flame kindle upon thee.- Isaiah 43:2

- Peace I leave with you, my peace I give unto you: not as the world giveth, give I unto you. Let not your heart be troubled, neither let it be afraid.- John 14:27

Filling Of Holy Spirit

- Turn you at my reproof: behold, I will pour out my Spirit unto you, I will make known my words unto you.- Proverbs 1:23

- For I will pour water upon him that is thirsty, and floods upon the dry ground: I will pour my Spirit upon thy seed, and my blessing upon thine offspring:- Isaiah 44:3

- And I say unto you, Ask, and it shall be given you; seek, and ye shall find; knock, and it shall be opened unto you. For every one that asketh receiveth; and he that seeketh findeth; and to him that knocketh it shall be opened. If a Son shall ask bread of any of you that is a Father, will he give him a stone? or if he ask a fish, will he for a fish give him a serpent? Or if he shall ask an egg, will he offer him a scorpion? If ye then, being evil, know how to give good gifts unto your children: how much more shall your heavenly Father give the Holy Spirit to them that ask him?- Luke 11:9-13

- And whatsoever ye shall ask in my name, that will I do, that the Father may be glorified in the Son. If ye shall ask any thing in my name, I will do it. If ye Love me, keep my commandments. And I will pray the Father, and he shall give you another Comforter, that he may abide with you forever;- John 14:13-16

- But ye shall receive power, after that the Holy Ghost is come upon you: and ye shall be witnesses unto me both in Jerusalem, and in all Judaea, and in Samaria, and unto the uttermost part of the earth.- Acts 1:8

- And it shall come to pass in the last days, saith God, I will pour out of my Spirit upon all flesh: and your sons and your daughters shall prophesy, and your young men shall see visions, and your old men shall dream dreams: And on my servants and on my handmaidens I will pour out in those days of my Spirit; and they shall prophesy:- Acts 2:17-18

- Then Peter said unto them, Repent, and be baptized every one of you in the name of Jesus Christ for the remission of sins, and ye shall receive the gift of the Holy Ghost. For the promise is unto you, and to your children, and to all that are afar off, even as many as the Lord our God shall call.- Acts 2:38-39

- That he would grant you, according to the riches of his glory, to be strengthened with might by his Spirit in the inner man; That Christ may dwell in your hearts by faith; that ye, being rooted and grounded in Love, May be able to comprehend with all saints what is the breadth, and length, and depth, and height; And to know the Love of Christ, which passeth knowledge, that ye might be filled with all the fullness of God.- Ephesians 3:16-19

Finances / Jobs

- The Lord shall open unto thee his good treasure, the Heaven to give the rain unto thy land in his season, and to bless all the work of thine hand: and thou shalt lend unto many nations, and thou shalt not borrow.- Deuteronomy 28:12

- Therefore take no thought, saying, What shall we eat? or, What shall we drink? or, Wherewithal shall we be clothed? (For after all these things do the Gentiles seek :) for your heavenly Father knoweth that ye have need of all these things. But seek ye first the kingdom of God, and his righteousness; and all these things shall be added unto you.- Matthew 6:31-33

- But my God shall supply all your need according to his riches in glory by Christ Jesus.- Philippians 4:19

Forgiveness

- If my people, which are called by my name, shall humble themselves, and pray, and seek my face, and turn from their wicked ways; then will I hear from Heaven, and will forgive their sin, and will heal their land.- 2 Chronicles 7:14

- Thou hast forgiven the iniquity of thy people, thou hast covered all their sin. Selah.- Psalms 85:2

- For thou, Lord, art good, and ready to forgive; and plenteous in mercy unto all them that call upon thee.- Psalms 86:5

- And when ye stand praying, forgive, if ye have ought against any: that your Father also which is in Heaven may forgive you your trespasses.- Mark 11:25

- And be ye kind one to another, tenderhearted, forgiving one another, even as God for Christ's sake hath forgiven you.- Ephesians 4:32

- If we confess our sins, he is faithful and just to forgive us our sins, and to cleanse us from all unrighteousness.- 1 John 1:9

Guidance

- And, behold, I am with thee, and will keep thee in all places whither thou goest, and will bring thee again into this land; for I will not leave thee, until I have done that which I have spoken to thee of.- Genesis 28:15

- What man is he that feareth the Lord? him shall he teach in the way that he shall choose.- Psalms 25:12

- I will instruct thee and teach thee in the way which thou shalt go: I will guide thee with mine eye.- Psalms 32:8

- Trust in the Lord with all thine heart; and lean not unto thine own understanding. In all thy ways acknowledge him, and he shall direct thy paths. Proverbs 3:5-6

- And if thou draw out thy soul to the hungry, and satisfy the afflicted soul; then shall thy light rise in obscurity, and thy darkness be as the noon day: And the Lord shall guide thee continually, and satisfy thy soul in drought, and make fat thy bones: and thou shalt be like a watered garden, and like a spring of water, whose waters fail not.- Isaiah 58:10-11

- And it shall come to pass, that before they call, I will answer; and while they are yet speaking, I will hear.- Isaiah 65:24

- Call unto me, and I will answer thee, and shew thee great and mighty things, which thou knowest not.- Jeremiah 33:3

- Howbeit when he, the Spirit of truth, is come, he will guide you into all truth: for he shall not speak of himself; but whatsoever he shall hear, that shall he speak: and he will shew you things to come.- John 16:13

- If any of you lack wisdom, let him ask of God, that giveth to all men liberally, and upbraideth not; and it shall be given him.- James 1:5

Health

- And said, If thou wilt diligently hearken to the voice of the Lord thy God, and wilt do that which is right in his sight, and wilt give ear to his commandments, and keep all his statutes, I will put none of these diseases upon thee, which I have brought upon the Egyptians: for I am the Lord that healeth thee.- Exodus 15:26

- Bless the Lord, O my soul, and forget not all his Benefits: Who forgiveth all thine iniquities; who healeth all thy diseases; Who redeemeth thy life from destruction; who crowneth thee with lovingkindness and tender mercies; Who satisfieth thy mouth with good things; so that thy youth is renewed like the eagle's.- Psalms 103:2-5

- Be not wise in thine own eyes: fear the Lord, and depart from evil. It shall be health to thy navel, and marrow to thy bones.- Proverbs 3:7-8

- But they that wait upon the Lord shall renew their strength; they shall mount up with wings as eagles; they shall run, and not be weary; and they shall walk, and not faint. Isaiah 40:31

- He is despised and rejected of men; a man of sorrows, and acquainted with grief: and we hid as it were our faces from him; he was despised, and we esteemed him not. Surely he hath borne our griefs, and carried our sorrows: yet we did esteem him stricken, smitten of God, and afflicted. But he was wounded for our transgressions, he was bruised for our iniquities: the chastisement of our peace was upon him; and with his stripes we are healed. Isaiah 53:3-5

- Heal me, O Lord, and I shall be healed; save me, and I shall be saved: for thou art my praise. Jeremiah 17:14

- For I will restore health unto thee, and I will heal thee of thy wounds, saith the Lord...Jeremiah 30:17

- But unto you that fear my name shall the Sun of righteousness arise with healing in his wings; and ye shall go forth, and grow up as calves of the stall. Malachi 4:2

- Is any sick among you? let him call for the elders of the church; and let them pray over him, anointing him with oil in the name of the Lord: And the prayer of faith shall save the sick, and the Lord shall raise him up; and if he hath committed sins, they shall be forgiven him. James 5:14-15

Marriage / Companionship

- And the Lord God said, It is not good that the man should be alone; I will make him an help meet for him. Genesis 2:18

- Delight thyself also in the Lord: and he shall give thee the desires of thine heart. Psalms 37:4

- God setteth the solitary in families..Psalms 68:6

- Whoso findeth a wife findeth a good thing, and obtaineth favour of the Lord. Proverbs 18:22

- For thy Maker is thine husband; the Lord of hosts is his name; and thy Redeemer the Holy One of Israel; The God of the whole earth shall he be called. Isaiah 54:5

- For I know the thoughts that I think toward you, saith the Lord, thoughts of peace, and not of evil, to give you an expected end. Jeremiah 29:11

- And this is the confidence that we have in him, that, if we ask any thing according to his will, he heareth us:1 John 5:14

Salvation / God's Love

- I have blotted out, as a thick cloud, thy transgressions, and, as a cloud, thy sins: return unto me; for I have redeemed thee. Isaiah 44:22

- And I will deliver thee out of the hand of the wicked, and I will redeem thee out of the hand of the terrible.Jeremiah 15:21

- For God so loved the world, that he gave his only begotten Son, that whosoever believeth in him should not perish, but have everlasting life. John 3:16

- He that believeth on the Son hath everlasting life: and he that believeth not the Son shall not see life; but the wrath of God abideth on him.
  John 3:36

- For the wages of sin is death; but the gift of God is eternal life through Jesus Christ our Lord. Romans 6:23

- For I am persuaded, that neither death, nor life, nor angels, nor principalities, nor powers, nor things present, nor things to come, Nor height, nor depth, nor any other creature, shall be able to separate us from the Love of God, which is in Christ Jesus our Lord. Romans 8:38-39

- That if thou shalt confess with thy mouth the Lord Jesus, and shalt believe in thine heart that God hath raised him from the dead, thou shalt be saved. For with the heart man believeth unto righteousness; and with the mouth confession is made unto salvation. Romans 10:9-10

- To the praise of the glory of his grace, wherein he hath made us accepted in the beloved. In whom we have redemption through his blood, the forgiveness of sins, according to the riches of his grace; Ephesians 1:6-7

- Let your conversation be without covetousness; and be content with such things as ye have: for he hath said, I will never leave thee, nor forsake thee. Hebrews 13:5

- If we confess our sins, he is faithful and just to forgive us our sins, and to cleanse us from all unrighteousness.1 John 1:9

- He that overcometh, the same shall be clothed in white raiment; and I will not blot out his name out of the book of life, but I will confess his name before my Father, and before his angels.Revelation 3:5

- Behold, I stand at the door, and knock: if any man hear my voice, and open the door, I will come in to him, and will sup with him, and he with me. Revelation 3:20

Strength To Do God's Will

- Have not I commanded thee? Be strong and of a good courage; be not afraid, neither be thou dismayed: for the Lord thy God is with thee whithersoever thou goest. Joshua 1:9

- Wait on the Lord: be of good courage, and he shall strengthen thine heart: wait, I say, on the Lord.Psalms 27:14

- He giveth power to the faint; and to them that have no might he increaseth strength. Isaiah 40:29

- No weapon that is formed against thee shall prosper; and every tongue that shall rise against thee in judgment thou shalt condemn. This is the heritage of the servants of the Lord, and their righteousness is of me, saith the Lord Isaiah 54:17

- A new heart also will I give you, and a new Spirit will I put within you: and I will take away the stony heart out of your flesh, and I will give you an heart of flesh. And I will put my Spirit within you, and cause you to walk-in my statutes, and ye shall keep my judgments, and do them. Ezekiel 36:26-27

- For which cause we faint not; but though our outward man perish, yet the inward man is renewed day by day. For our light affliction, which is but for a moment, worketh for us a far more exceeding and eternal weight of glory; While we look not at the things which are seen, but at the things which are not seen: for the things which are seen are temporal; but the things which are not seen are eternal. 2 Corinthians 4:16-18

- And let us not be weary in well doing: for in due season we shall reap, if we faint not. Galatians 6:9

- I can do all things through Christ which strengtheneth me. Philippians 4:13

www.ingramcontent.com/pod-product-compliance
Lightning Source LLC
Chambersburg PA
CBHW022246290526
45785CB00015B/371